THE PRINCIPALSHIP

BUILDING A LEARNING COMMUNITY

D1539427

Marsha Speck
San Jose State University

THE
PRINCIPALSHIP

BUILDING
A LEARNING
COMMUNITY

Merrill
an imprint of Prentice Hall

Upper Saddle River, New Jersey
Columbus, Ohio

Library of Congress Cataloging-in-Publication Data

Speck, Marsha.
  The principalship : building a learning community / by Marsha Speck.
     p.   cm.
  Includes bibliographical references and index.
  ISBN 0-13-440686-9
  1. School principals—Training of. 2. School management and organiza-
tion. 3. Community and school. 4. Problem-based learning.   I. Title.
  LB1738.5.S64   1999
  371.2'012—dc21   98-26326
                                                                     CIP

Cover art: © Proof Positive
Editor: Debra A. Stollenwerk
Production Editor: Linda Hillis Bayma
Design Coordinator: Diane C. Lorenzo
Text Designer: Pagination
Cover Designer: Proof Positive/Kathy Horning
Production Manager: Pamela D. Bennett
Electronic Text Management: Marilyn Wilson Phelps, Karen L. Bretz,
    Tracey B. Ward
Illustrations: Tom Kennedy
Director of Marketing: Kevin Flanagan
Marketing Manager: Suzanne Stanton
Advertising/Marketing Coordinator: Krista Groshong

This book was set in Century Schoolbook by Prentice Hall and was printed and
bound by R.R. Donnelley & Sons Company. The cover was printed by Phoenix
Color Corp.

© 1999 by Prentice-Hall, Inc.
Simon & Schuster/A Viacom Company
Upper Saddle River, New Jersey 07458

Printed in the United States of America

10 9 8 7 6 5 4 3 2 1

ISBN: 0-13-440686-9

Prentice-Hall International (UK) Limited, *London*
Prentice-Hall of Australia Pty. Limited, *Sydney*
Prentice-Hall of Canada, Inc., *Toronto*
Prentice-Hall Hispanoamericana, S. A., *Mexico*
Prentice-Hall of India Private Limited, *New Delhi*
Prentice-Hall of Japan, Inc., *Tokyo*
Simon & Schuster Asia Pte. Ltd., *Singapore*
Editora Prentice-Hall do Brasil, Ltda., *Rio de Janeiro*

To the many dedicated

principals, teachers, staff,

students, parents, and

communities that I have

worked with over the years

who, faced with obstacles,

have continually worked at

developing learning

communities within their

schools to benefit the quality

of learning and life for all.

PREFACE

Given the many demands on the principalship and the influences of change on schools, I have written this text to meet the needs of prospective principals who can help schools become learning communities. Developing a school where learning is nourished by every aspect of the school community, by everyone who comes in contact with the school and contributes to the learning community, is an important concept upon which a principal must build. As a recent practicing principal and a professor of educational leadership, I have tried to offer a balanced approach, blending practical experience and the theoretical knowledge needed to develop educational leaders. *The Principalship: Building a Learning Community* provides a problem-based approach to learning about the principalship and building learning communities within our schools.

The Principalship Model, introduced and explained in the text, provides a framework to explore the principal's multidimensional roles as educator, leader, manager, and inner person in today's school learning community. The student of the principalship can begin to define these roles of the principal and understand the abilities and skills a successful principal must possess.

ORGANIZATION OF THE TEXT

Each chapter begins with a problem scenario and follows with the knowledge base from which students can develop possible solution(s) to the problem. Reflective activities are provided at the end of each chapter and give the student an opportunity to extend their learning about concepts explored in the chapter. Students can use these reflective activities within their district or school to extend their learning about the principalship.

NOTE TO THE READER

Please take the time to focus on the problem scenario in the beginning of each chapter. The problem scenario sets the stage for the reader's inquiry and focused thoughts in preparation for reading a chapter. Take the time to write down your thoughts surrounding the problem scenario and review your written ideas after reading the chapter. Through this reflective practice, students of the principalship will develop habits of inquiry and reflection that will sustain their continuous growth as educators and leaders for improving our schools.

ACKNOWLEDGMENTS

The Principalship: Building a Learning Community has been inspired by my work with so many principals, teachers, staff, students, parents, and community members as well as my university colleagues, especially Marty Krovetz and William Zachmeier. I would like to thank each of them for the clarifying insights and experiences I have gained as a principal and colleague in the work of building our schools into learning communities that make a difference for student achievement. I am grateful for the thoughtful comments of the reviewers who helped clarify critical issues raised in the text: Martha Bruckner, University of Nebraska at Omaha; James A. Burchett, Miami University; Glenn I. Earthman, Virginia Polytechnic Institute and State University; David A. Erlandson, Texas A&M University; Gene Gallegos, California State University, Bakersfield; Larry W. Hughes, University of Houston; Rebecca W. Libler, Indiana State University; James S. Rinehart, University of Kentucky; and Frederick C. Wendel, University of Nebraska at Lincoln.

Finally, I want to thank Debbie Stollenwerk, my editor at Merrill/Prentice Hall, for her faith and undaunted encouragement in my ability and experience to write this book. Thanks to the excellent and diligent work of Linda Bayma, production editor, and Linda Belew, copy editor, the text comes to life and expresses what it is to develop schools into learning communities. And sincere thanks to Sue Webber for seeing me through the early stages of proofing and the entire process.

BRIEF CONTENTS

CONTENTS

THE PRINCIPALSHIP

BUILDING A LEARNING COMMUNITY

CHAPTER 1

BUILDING A LEARNING COMMUNITY —THE PRINCIPALSHIP

PROBLEM SCENARIO

You have just been appointed principal of Hope School. As a new principal in an unfamiliar school community, you are anxious to succeed at building a learning community within the school. The school community is excited to have you as its new leader and principal, especially after the last two principals who proved ineffective and were removed by the Board of Education. Students, teachers, staff, parents, and other members of the community want to know who you are and what plans you have as principal for building a school learning community. What does the principalship mean to you? How will you put your leadership into action as the new principal of Hope School? What does it mean to build a community of learners within your school?

BUILDING A SCHOOL LEARNING COMMUNITY

Schools should foster learning not only for students, but also for all adults in the community—teachers, staff, principal, parents, and others—creating a community of learners. Building a learning community is the most important and demanding responsibility of the principalship. A principal should not be just a school keeper but must develop a community of learners within the school environment. Creating a school that serves all learners cannot be accomplished by the solitary actions of a principal. It results from a systematic building of collegiality and community through an atmosphere of ongoing learning for all members of the school community. Providing and increasing learning for all students requires the determined collaboration of the key figures in each student's life.

Few schools today succeed at meeting the diverse needs of their students and providing the best education possible for all students. There is a real need to address what a school should be as a learning community and determine how to stop the isolated actions of teachers, principal, and staff, who view their work as "my kids," "my classes," "my classroom," "my school"—with classroom doors shut and no evidence of sharing or true collegial interaction. Have you seen a school community whose members have developed a collective sense of learning together, sharing ideas and growing, and generating enthusiasm for shared learning between and among students, teachers, principals, staff, parents, and the entire school community? How would you describe that school learning community? Can you picture that school learning community with you as the principal?

In *Horace's Hope* (1996) Sizer writes that principals need to evolve from the craft of school keeping, with its incessant and fascinating dailiness, and pursue change in ways somewhat different from traditional reform activities (p. xii). The principal must deal with the stability in public education that comes from the extraordinary inertia of traditional practice. Bold changes for a school require sustained leadership of the principal to involve and nurture the collective learning of those who hold a stake in the school (teachers, students, staff, parents, and community) to improve the learning for each student. How does the principal move from school keeping to building a community of learners that serves all students?

The principalship has evolved into multidimensional roles: **leader, educator, manager,** and **inner person** (Speck 1995). These complex and interrelated roles define how the principal helps develop and foster a true school learning community where the entire school community (teachers, staff, principal, students, and parents) develops habits of continual learning (study, plan, act, reflect, and refine learning as a cycle). The essence of principalship is creating a collaborative school where learning really matters and the community of learners cares deeply about each student's achievement. A **school learning community** is one in which students learn to use their minds well, and the adults and students model that practice every day throughout the school.

Schools for thoughtfulness can't be built on top of thoughtlessness. (Meier 1995, 35)

In *The Power of Their Ideas* (1995) Meier describes her work at Central Park East schools (CPESS), where both adults and students must develop and model important habits of mind:

CPESS focuses on five major "intellectual habits"—habits that should be internalized by every student, and used no matter what they are studying about, both in school and especially out of it! These five "habits" include concern for evidence (how do you know that?), viewpoint (who said it and why?), cause and effect (what led to it, what else happened?), and hypothesizing (what if, supposing that?). But most important of all is the fifth "habit": who cares? (p. 41)

The school learning community is the fiber and soul of the school through which continuous learning takes place. The school reflects on its actions to improve learning for all students through constant, engaged dialogue about what is important for students to know and be able to do. This practice is hardly the norm in most schools. Generally, teachers are isolated within their classrooms and merely chat at lunch about events not related to school. Many schools have this sort of congenial, or socially friendly, environment, but they lack the collegial spirit that is essential for a learning community (Barth 1990). How can a school evolve to become a learning community that challenges, supports, and cares about learning for all students and adults associated with the school?

I think that the problem of how to change things from "I" to "we," of how to bring a good measure of collegiality and relateness to adults who work in schools, is one that belongs on the national agenda of school improvement—at the top. It belongs at the top because the relationships among adults in schools are the basis, the precondition, the *sine qua non* that allow, energize, and sustain all other attempts at school improvement. Unless adults talk with one another, observe one another, and help one another, very little will change.[1]

The principal plays a pivotal role in building a learning commu-nity (Barth 1990; Glickman 1993; Sergiovanni 1996, 1994; Sizer 1996). The principal must lead the efforts of change while overcoming the details and daily routines of merely keeping school. The goal of creat-ing a learning community within the school is too important to be left to chance. Without strong leadership, the goal will not even exist in

---

[1] Reprinted with permission of Jossey-Bass Inc. from *Improving Schools from Within*, 32, by Roland Barth. © 1990 by Jossey-Bass Inc., Publishers.

most schools. As an individual takes on the role of the principalship and works at building a learning community, there is a critical need to focus on four key questions.

Key Questions for the Principal in Building a Learning Community

1.	What is a school learning community?
2.	How will a learning community affect students and their achievements, teachers, staff, the principal, and the community as a whole?
3.	Who is involved and what are the processes they must follow in building a learning community?
4.	What multidimensional roles does the principal play in building the learning community?

REFLECTIONS: PAUSE FOR A MOMENT AND WRITE DOWN YOUR REFLECTIONS ON THESE KEY QUESTIONS.

KEY QUESTION 1: WHAT IS A SCHOOL LEARNING COMMUNITY?

Serious discussion of creating learning communities began in the corporate world, rather than the school community. Why is that? In *The Fifth Discipline* (1990) Senge suggests that the corporate world needs to create learning organizations that destroy the illusion that the world is created of separate, unrelated forces and foster the concept that people can continually expand their learning together to benefit the larger organization. Senge states:

> When we give up this illusion . . . we can then build "learning organizations," organizations where people continually expand their capacity to create the results they truly desire, where new and expansive patterns of thinking are nurtured, where collective aspiration is set free, and where people are continually learning how to learn together.[2]

[2] Reprinted with permission of Doubleday from *The Fifth Discipline: The Art and Practice of the Learning Organization*, 3, by Peter Senge. © 1990 by Doubleday.

The corporate world views learning organizations, described by Senge (1990), as a means of continual survival in the economic marketplace for corporations where continuous learning together is valued in order to keep the corporation competitive and exact profits for shareholders. The learning organization evolves and can deal with the problems and opportunities of today, as well as invest in its capacity to embrace tomorrow, because its members are focused on enhancing and expanding their collective awareness and capabilities—creating an organization that can learn (Senge et al. 1994). People in learning organizations look forward to creating the new world that is emerging, instead of merely reacting to it. As learning organizations, are our schools creating or merely reacting to the world of the future that our students will face? Are our schools learning organizations at all?

According to Senge (O'Neil 1995), an organization's ability to learn may make the difference between its thriving or perishing in the years ahead. Senge (O'Neil 1995) does not see schools as learning organizations, as noted in his response to this question: Schools are considered to be institutions of learning, but are most of them learning organizations?

> [Are most schools learning organizations?] Definitely not. A learning organization is an organization in which people at all levels are, collectively, continually enhancing their capacity to create things they really want to create. And most of the educators I talk with don't feel like they're doing this. Most teachers feel oppressed trying to conform to all kinds of rules, goals and objectives, many of which they don't believe in. Teachers don't work together; there's very little sense of collective learning going on in most schools. (p. 20)

Given the impetus from the business world for creating learning organizations and what is known about the school as an organization, what is a school learning community? A school learning community is one that promotes and values learning as an ongoing, active collaborative process with dynamic dialogue by teachers, students, staff, principal, parents, and the school community to improve the quality of learning and life within the school. Developing schools where every aspect of the community nourishes learning and helping everyone who comes in contact with the school to contribute to that learning community are important concepts.

REFLECTIONS: DOES A LEARNING COMMUNITY EXIST WITHIN
....
YOUR CURRENT SCHOOL? WHY OR WHY NOT? TAKE TIME TO
....
WRITE DOWN YOUR THOUGHTS.

Several noted authors have discussed the concept of a learning community in education. Barth (1990), in *Improving Schools from Within,* describes a picture of a school learning community:

Central to my conception of a good school and a healthy workplace is community. In particular, I would want to return to work in a school that could be described as a community of learners, a place where students and adults alike are engaged as active learners in matters of special importance to them and where everyone is thereby encouraging everyone else's learning. And I would readily work in a school that could be described as a community of leaders, where students, teachers, parents, and administrators share the opportunities and responsibilities for making decisions that affect all the occupants of the schoolhouse.[3]

In *The Basic School,* the Carnegie Foundation's work on the elementary school, Boyer (1995) states:

The Basic School has, as the first requirement, a clear and vital mission. The school is a place where everyone comes together to promote learning. Every classroom is, itself, a community. But in the Basic School, the separate classrooms are connected by a sense of purpose, in a climate that is communicative, just, disciplined, and caring, with occasions for celebration. The Basic School is, above all else, a community for learning, a place where staff and students, along with parents, have a shared vision of what the institution is seeking to accomplish. There is simply no way to achieve educational excellence in a school where purposes are blurred, where teachers and students fail to communicate thoughtfully with each other, and where parents are uninvolved in the education of their children. Community is, without question, the glue that holds an effective school together.[4]

Schools and classrooms, as isolated fortresses, have not really invited the true spirit of a learning community to exist. Why does this condition exist?

Prawat (1993) sees the goal of learning communities as building social and intellectual connections among people to define a shared understanding of what they are about and what they are trying to accomplish. The metaphor of the learning community explains the thoughts of constructivism where individuals are given time, ideas,

---

[3] Reprinted with permission of Jossey-Bass Inc. from *Improving Schools from Within,* 9, by Roland Barth. © 1990 by Jossey-Bass Inc., Publishers.

[4] Reprinted with permission of The Carnegie Foundation for Advancement of Teaching from *The Basic School: A Community for Learning,* 15, by Ernest L. Boyer. © 1995 by The Carnegie Foundation for Advancement of Teaching.

and interactions to construct their own knowledge and learning. As Prawat's (1993) statement explains:

> Current research on learning . . . has changed the focus of our attention in education—away from an individual differences approach in teaching and toward one that focuses on developing a learning community in the classroom. (p. 8)

It is constructivism that looks at the work of teachers not as delivering good lessons but as being able to create a classroom learning community (Prawat 1992, 12). Building on this idea, it is the work of the principal, along with others, to make the entire school a learning community. Schools should be places where not only students are learners but where every adult is also engaged in learning, including teachers, principal, staff, and other adults in the community.

Sergiovanni's *Leadership for the Schoolhouse* (1996) elaborates on the school as a learning community:

> I believe that a theory for the schoolhouse should provide for decisions about school organization and functioning, curriculum, and classroom life that reflect constructivist teaching and learning principles. I believe that a theory of the schoolhouse should strive to transform the school into a center of inquiry—a place where professional knowledge is created in use as teachers learn together, solve problems together, and inquire together. (p. 27)

A school learning community must be invented by each school and principal working together based on democratic principles and frameworks, some of which are cited in this book. Each school learning community will be unique, but it will still have common threads with other school learning communities. In the process of developing the learning community, the school and principal must take on the challenge of making it real for their school. A school learning community has a sense of interdependency, mutual obligations, commitments, and love of learning. These forces combine to enhance learning and quality of life not only for students but for every member of the learning community.

In *Building Community in Schools,* Sergiovanni (1994) states that the defining characteristics of schools as communities are the special ways that people bond together and their connections to shared values and ideas (p. 4). Communities are defined by their centers of values, sentiments, and beliefs that provide the needed conditions for creating a sense of "we" from "I." School learning communities have the values of shared learning, teaching, reflection, planning, acting, and ongoing reflection and dialogue that focus on improving achievement for students and all other members of the learning community.

In a school learning community, learning is promoted and valued as an ongoing, active, collaborative, collegial process that includes dynamic dialogues that get at the heart of schooling and learning to improve the quality of learning and life for all members of the school community.

The role of the principalship is vital in developing a school learning community. Senge (O'Neil 1995) reinforces the importance of the role of the principal, within the school learning organization, as helping create an environment for continual learning that is collaborative and directed at the learner. The principal must foster a school learning environment where the learning community grows and flourishes as a whole, rather than individual students or classrooms. Senge (O'Neil 1995) points out common aspects of learning in business and education:

> Our fundamental challenges in education are no different than in business. They involve fundamental cultural changes, and that will require collective learning. They involve people at multiple levels thinking together about significant and enduring solutions we might create, and helping those solutions come about. (p. 21)

The school learning community must engage in critical, essential questions that define the quality of learning and life for the school. In the leadership role, the principal must help bring about significant changes through dialogue and other efforts that foster learning throughout the school.

REFLECTIONS: AS A PRINCIPAL, WHAT WOULD BE THE CRITICAL, ESSENTIAL QUESTIONS FOR YOUR SCHOOL THAT DEFINE THE QUALITY OF LEARNING AND LIFE WITHIN THE SCHOOL LEARNING COMMUNITY? HOW WOULD YOU BRING PEOPLE TOGETHER TO ADDRESS THESE QUESTIONS? TAKE TIME TO WRITE DOWN YOUR THOUGHTS.

This book provides a framework for answering these critical questions about building a learning community and the principalship. The principal has a key role in defining and developing the school learning community through helping the school define and answer the essential questions it must address. Questions that help a school define the quality of learning and life within a school learning community are posed here and discussed in detail in Chapter 7.

Essential Questions: Defining the Quality of Learning and Life Within a School Learning Community

What do we want students to know and be able to do?

What kinds of learning experiences produce these outcomes?

How will we know that students can do these things?

What does it take to transform schools into places where this happens?

Who is responsible for ensuring that the desired results are achieved?

Unless the principal develops a school culture that inquires into these essential questions for defining the quality of learning and life within a school community, there will be no change in the current school from an isolated, fragmented institution where the full potential for learning does not exist. This leads to the next key question for the principal to focus on in building a learning community.

KEY QUESTION 2: HOW WILL A LEARNING COMMUNITY AFFECT STUDENTS AND THEIR ACHIEVEMENTS, TEACHERS, STAFF, THE PRINCIPAL, AND THE COMMUNITY AS A WHOLE?

If successful, a learning community will alter many aspects of life for all members—students and their achievements, teachers, staff, the principal, and the community as a whole. The effect will be demonstrated by a deep sense of learning, continuous growth, and success for each member and through the daily interactions that model continuous learning. Chapter 7 will discuss curriculum, instruction, and assessment, providing specific examples of how they will affect the achievements of a learning community's members.

KEY QUESTION 3: WHO IS INVOLVED AND WHAT ARE THE PROCESSES THEY MUST FOLLOW IN BUILDING A LEARNING COMMUNITY?

A learning community involves all who hold a stake in the outcome: teachers, staff, students, principal, parents, and the rest of the community. The principal is not the sole designer of the learning community but is the facilitator and creator of ongoing dialogue with the various stakeholders. Together they develop and generate a community of learners. The daily building of a learning community is the thousands of dialogues that take place within the school one-on-one, one-on-two, one-on-three, etc. that occur every day. A principal must lead by walking, talking, and facilitating conversations about students' work, including their successes and their failures, with teachers, students, staff, parents, and others in the community every day. The role of the principal in building the learning community through stakeholder involvement is developed in Part II of this book (Chapters 6 through 11). As the reader will see, the processes for developing a learning community are unique to each school.

KEY QUESTION 4: WHAT MULTIDIMENSIONAL ROLES DOES THE PRINCIPAL PLAY IN BUILDING THE LEARNING COMMUNITY?

Given the ever-changing demands on the school, the influences of reform, restructuring, change, and the need to build learning communities within schools, there is a need to explore the multidimensional roles of the principalship. The principalship is the key leadership position in the improvement of education for all students. Although the principal can and should not be seen as the sole instructional leader of the school, the principal is the keeper of the vision. Principals must promote continuous learning not only for students, but also for teachers, staff, parents, and others in the community as well as themselves. The principal can facilitate building the learning community within the school by developing and fostering collegiality and collaboration in a variety of ways so that they become a part of the school's culture. The principal cannot be isolated from the faculty, but must facilitate and encourage an ongoing process of learning together within and without the school.

The principalship's multidimensional roles (see Figure 1.1 on page 18)—educator, leader, manager, and inner person—are the focus of this book and will be touched on briefly in this chapter. The Principalship Model will be clarified in Part I of this book (Chapters 2 through 5).

The influencing processes and elements of the Principalship Model will be dealt with through answers to the key questions for the principal in building a learning community in Part II (Chapters 6 through 11).

Thus, the principalship presents challenging questions about building a learning community to each person who seeks the position. The guidelines on processes and multidimensional roles in developing a learning community should help new principals deal with typical concerns as stated by Barth (1990):

> The loneliness of the position is more than I expected. I hadn't expected the distance between teachers and between teachers and myself. While I knew there would be some distance, I expected to be playing on the same team and working together. In fact, teachers are not comfortable with the principal entering the coffee room.

I find that there are few people to share information with and who seem to have similar concerns and problems. Need it be so?[5]

REFLECTIONS: AS A NEW OR PRACTICING PRINCIPAL, DOES THE ABOVE DESCRIPTION NEED TO BE TRUE? HOW WOULD YOU AS A PRINCIPAL DEVELOP A TRUE SCHOOL LEARNING COMMUNITY THAT MAKES A DIFFERENCE FOR STUDENTS, TEACHERS, STAFF, PARENTS, AND THE COMMUNITY AS A WHOLE? TAKE TIME TO WRITE DOWN YOUR THOUGHTS.

THE PRINCIPALSHIP—RECENT PERSPECTIVES

The principalship continues to change and has gained attention for making the difference in a school's success. In reviewing various studies on school effectiveness, Austin (cited in Smith and Piele 1996, 4) summarized factors that distinguished effective schools from others, revealing the importance of the role of the principal in effective schools:

- Principals provided strong leadership (for example, schools being run for a purpose rather than "running from force of habit").
- Principals participated extensively in the classroom instructional program and even in teaching.
- Principals had higher expectations for student and teacher advancement.
- Principals felt that they had more control over the functioning of the school, the curriculum and program, and their staff.

Edmonds' (1979) studies reveal that the most indispensable characteristic of effective schools is strong administrative leadership, without which the disparate elements of good schooling can neither be brought

[5] Reprinted with permission of Jossey-Bass Inc. from *Improving Schools from Within*, 26, by Roland Barth. © 1990 by Jossey-Bass Inc., Publishers.

together nor kept together. In Edmonds' view, leadership is not only important, but it is the single most important factor in school effectiveness.

Since the effective school studies and the considerable effort that
has been devoted to restructuring in the last ten years, several authors
have observed that the role of the principal quite often is very different
from the role described in the effective schools research. The role is
evolving from the characterization of the principal as a strong, forceful
leader who provided the impetus for change and improvement with the
school by dint of personality alone (Goldman, Dunlap, and Conley 1993;
Louis 1992; Prestine 1991). In restructuring schools, principals demonstrate such skills as leading through and with others, not by dictating
but by facilitating. Discussing ways in which principals in the Coalition
of Essential Schools exercise power, Cushman (1992) highlights the
movement away from some tenets of the effective schools research:

> Researchers within the Coalition of Essential Schools argue . . .
> that the Effective Schools model is less well suited for schools mov-
> ing away from the existing system. They see that system as flawed,
> along with the convention of one strong leader it depends on. (p. 2)

Short and Greer (1997) and Beck and Murphy (1996) reinforce a
new definition of the principalship as one of empowering others, facilitating, and relinquishing control of decision making. The principal's
facilitative leadership, participatory decision making, and problem-
solving teamwork provide for interaction and empowerment that lead
to more collegial and intensifying interactions between all parties in an
empowered school (Short and Greer 1997; Lambert et al. 1995). Recent
studies have found that the principal's role includes resource finder,
facilitator, shared-decision maker, innovative thinker, and student
advocate. The principal functions as the "conscience of the school,"
providing a continuing focus on students. The principal's actions and
decisions are guided by a vision of education (Conley 1993). The vision
may reside in the principal as an individual, but more frequently it is
created jointly with the staff; in all cases this vision is clearly and
repeatedly articulated within the school learning community.

Most importantly, the principal is the school **facilitative leader**
who brings together all the stakeholders in the school community to help
create a learning community for students, teachers, staff, parents, and
the community. The principal makes the difference in the learning
and lives of all who come in contact with the school. The responsibility and
obligation of the principalship to build a learning community is vital. The
variety of individual students and the ever-changing society dramatize
the need for a good education founded in a school that cares and provides
a learning experience, making a real difference in preparing students for
success as citizens and continuous learners.

REFLECTIONS: HOW DOES AN EDUCATOR PREPARE FOR THE PRIN-

....

CIPALSHIP? WHAT ROLES AND SKILLS WILL BE NEEDED FOR THE

....

PRINCIPALSHIP? TAKE TIME TO WRITE DOWN YOUR THOUGHTS.

THE PRINCIPALSHIP MODEL

Today the principalship is dynamic, complex, and demanding. The constancy of change affects the position of the principalship. As we enter the twenty-first century, what does it take to be a principal in today's schools where learning communities are desperately needed? Exploration of the multidimensional roles of the principalship in building a learning community will offer important insights. There is a need to gain perspectives on the roles a principal must take to demonstrate leading, educating, managing, and keeping a balanced inner person for creating a learning community (Speck 1995). The multidimensional, integrated roles of the principalship (educator, leader, manager, and inner person) will be explained here to provide the conceptual basis for the principalship model used in this book. The Principalship Model (Figure 1.1) will provide the framework for understanding the principalship and creating a school learning community including collaborative processes and factors shared throughout the book. Through this exploration, the student of the principalship can begin to define the roles of the principal and begin to develop an understanding of the abilities and skills needed to become a successful principal as a learning community grows.

The old ways of doing things in schools must change to meet the changing needs of the school community and its students. With the vast diversity of student needs and our changing society, the principal cannot simply maintain the traditional roles of the past. The principal must continually develop skills and strategies to move the school toward success for all students, no matter what the school's current situation happens to be. Today, the principal is not the only educational manager, leader, and educator in the school. The creation of a learning community requires the principal to reexamine, redefine, and expand the multiple roles as principal. The principal must provide the facilitative leadership that will make a difference in the lives of children and refuse to accept the mediocrity and failure rates that exist in many of our nation's schools. According to Sergiovanni (1995):

> In the actual world of schooling, the task of the principal is to make
> sense of messy situations by increasing understanding and discover-

ing and communicating meanings. . . . Uncertainty and complexity are normal aspects in the process of schooling. (pp. 31–32)

REFLECTIONS: WHAT ARE THE PRINCIPAL'S ROLES WITHIN THE

PRINCIPALSHIP MODEL, AND HOW ARE THEY INFLUENCED TO

BUILD A LEARNING COMMUNITY? WRITE DOWN YOUR THOUGHTS.

ROLES IN THE PRINCIPALSHIP MODEL

The principalship and its variety of roles are dynamic and fluid with the melding of educational, management, leadership, and the balance of the inner person skills, providing overall leadership for building a school into a learning community for all students. The Principalship Model (Figure 1.1) depicts these relationships with an overview of the principalship and the balance of roles and skills necessary for a successful leader and principal: educator, manager, leader, and inner person. The principal is the chief architect of building a school learning community where all parties who interact in the school community come together for learning.

Following is an introduction to each of the roles in the **Principalship Model**, providing the reader with an overview of these roles and the important skills needed for a principal to succeed. This chapter also presents the key factors that influence the principal's success in building a learning community. The rest of this book elaborates on each role and factor, thus reinforcing the Principalship Model and related practices.

The principal must take on and continue to develop the **educator role** (Figure 1.2) by clearly understanding current research and practices in the areas of student characteristics and needs; the development, implementation, and evaluation of curriculum and instruction; the improvement of school climate; and the organization and improvement of student services, including student progress monitoring and reporting. The educator's role is the instructional leadership aspect where the principal, along with the teachers, develops the appropriate curriculum, instruction, and assessments that will help all students in the school succeed to their full potential. The principal collaboratively builds the vision and communicates the educational focus of the school. It is important for a principal to understand the educator role

FIGURE 1.1

The Principalship
Model

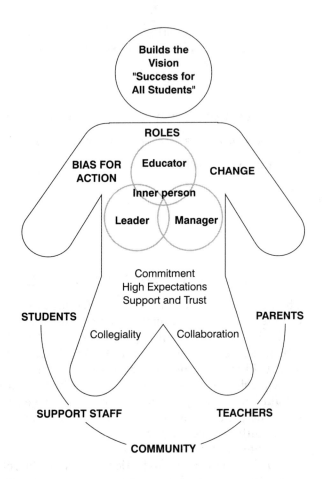

clearly and use it to build a learning community. Chapter 2 will provide a more in-depth view of the educator role in the Principalship Model.

In the **role of leader** (Figure 1.3), the principal must be able to appraise the present, anticipate the future, and help develop a school vision in collaboration with the various school stakeholders. For the principal, the leadership role provides for determining the capacity for change, as well as planning and implementing change, including assessing individual and group capacities for change. The leader role requires the principal to select and practice appropriate leadership styles in different settings and provide a clear focus. Empowering staff and students, building trust, monitoring and assessing progress, and providing assistance are critical elements of the leader role in the principalship. As a leader, the principal must show appreciation and celebrate accomplishments. Taking care of the students, staff, and community should become a clear focus for the principal. Motivating people, including the school community, is an important part of the leader role that calls for interpersonal and group skills. Chapter 3 will elaborate on the leader role in the Principalship Model.

The **manager role** (Figure 1.4) for a principal includes preparing, planning, organizing, carrying out, and directing overall school operations as well as monitoring an evaluation process for continued improvement of the school. The principal must develop the ability to manage recurring functions of the school through management systems that provide for an effective and efficiently run school. The principal, as manager, means taking care of the daily tasks that keep the school running and providing for a work environment where teachers, staff, and students can carry out their teaching and learning. It's the management operations of a school that the principal must grasp in order for the basic school learning environment to be established. It's the management specifics of buses, bells, books, budgets, lunches, custodial services, and reporting systems that create certain management conditions that principals must direct for the effective operation of the school. Without the fundamentals of management, the principal can not carry out the multidimensional roles—the school would be in chaos. Chapter 4 will explore the manager role in the Principalship Model in greater detail.

The **inner person** is a term used to describe the personal beliefs and internal balance that the principal needs to keep while carrying out the role on a daily basis. The inner person role in the Principalship Model (Figure 1.5) asks that principals clarify beliefs about how people learn, where they stand on social issues affecting schools and the

---

Educator Role

- Continues to study, learn, and reflect on practice
- Builds a vision and communicates educational focus
- Reviews research and exemplary programs
- Helps conduct and promote collaborative action research
- Understands students and their needs
- Develops, aligns, implements, and evaluates curriculum and instruction
- Improves school climate and culture
- Organizes and improves student services
- Monitors students' progress

FIGURE 1.2
The Principal as Educator

FIGURE 1.3
The Principal as
Leader

Leader Role

- Appraises the present
- Envisions the future
- Communicates the vision
- Determines capacity for change
- Plans and implements change
- Deploys self
- Empowers staff and community
- Builds trust
- Monitors and assesses progress
- Shows appreciation and celebrates accomplishments
- Takes care of staff, students, and community
- Motivates members of the school community
- Uses human skills (interpersonal and group)

school community, and their personal educational philosophy. The inner person role is intertwined with the educator role because it provides the foundation for what one believes and does as a principal. Issues of ethical, honest, and humane actions are raised within the inner person as well as the practice of good habits of physical and emotional wellness for a principal. Through the inner person aspect of the Principalship Model, the principal should enjoy family and friends, plan for financial security, read widely, participate culturally in the community, tolerate an ambiguous world, tap inner resources of personal strengths, and keep a sense of humor and amazement of the edu-

FIGURE 1.4
The Principal as
Manager

Manager Role

- Prepares
- Plans
- Organizes
- Manages through recurring systems
- Directs and carries out
- Evaluates and improves

FIGURE 1.5
The Principal as
Inner Person

Inner Person

- Clarifies beliefs about schooling and learning
- Is committed to schooling and learning
- Acts ethically and honestly
- Practices good habits of physical and emotional wellness
- Balances life
- Plans for financial security
- Enjoys family, friends, and social/cultural activities
- Reads widely and keeps professionally updated
- Reflects on practice
- Tolerates an ambiguous world
- Taps inner resources for strength and humor

cational world as it unfolds. Chapter 4 will take a closer look at the inner person role in the Principalship Model.

KEY FACTORS SURROUNDING THE PRINCIPALSHIP MODEL

BIAS FOR ACTION

Principals rarely have the luxury of contemplating a decision for very long because of the pace of change and the demands of tending to the diverse needs of the many high-risk children who attend the school. Principals must have a **bias for action** (Peters and Waterman 1981; Fullan 1988, 1993) if they expect to succeed at changing the school into a learning community that values and makes a difference in each student's life. It is in a bias for action that the school's vision and mission are communicated to all the stakeholders and make a difference in the student's education. Analysis of data and a clear collaborative decision-making process provide for a bias for action that communicates the leadership of the principal to the school community. A principal who does not produce positive outcomes for students and the school will not survive long in any community. As Fullan (1988) describes it:

Recent evidence in both business and education indicates that effective leaders have a "bias for action." They have an overall sense of direction and start into action as soon as possible, establishing small-scale examples, adapting, refining, improving quality, expanding, and reshaping as the process unfolds. This strategy might be summed up as *start small, think big;* or the way to get better at implementation planning is more by doing than by planning. (p. 27)

The research on the principalship by Murphy (1994), Beck and Murphy (1996), and Short and Greer (1997) clearly portrays the principal in action as an administrator who performs multiple tasks superficially in a brief duration of time in a fragmentary manner—a fragmented superficiality, as Beck and Murphy describe it. The ability to deal with varied and unrelated events in a random, rapid-fire way describes the daily life of the principal. Therefore, it is important for the person in the principalship to have a clear focus on priorities to make a successful school. Successful principals have a passion for schooling and frequently test the limits of the current system to make a real difference in the student's education. This overriding commitment to students' learning, teachers, and the school guides the principal's actions each day. Watching any successful principal will convince you that actions speak louder than words.

THE CHANGE PROCESS

Initiating change in a school learning community does not just happen, nor does institutionalizing the changes. It is critical for principals to understand the change process (Fullan 1993) as they develop a school learning community. The Principalship Model helps principals understand the critical elements of the change process (Chapter 11) and how to sustain systematic change within the school.

INFLUENCES AND CORE BELIEFS

The Principalship Model portrays students, teachers, support staff, parents, and community as interwoven. The core beliefs of the Principalship Model are commitment with caring, high expectations with appropriate support, and participation and involvement through collegiality and collaboration. Members of the learning community develop trust by the quality of daily interactions with the principal and with one another.

The surrounding environment of the school must show commitment and collaboration with all stakeholders (teachers, staff, students, principal, parents, and community). Commitment and collaboration must be based on a firm foundation of high expectations with support and trust. Collegiality of the teachers, staff, and principal develops with interaction on a daily basis, discussing issues of importance that stimulate the habits of minds within the school. Learning communities do not exist without commitment, collaborative, and collegial processes, all supported by the trust of the stakeholders. Communities for learning within schools are built daily by the lively interaction of active involvement and participation of the stakeholders working to improve the quality of learning within the school.

As you study the principalship, this model will help you analyze how well you are functioning in each role—educator, leader, manager, and inner person—and identify the influencing factors. Use the model as a guide for your understanding of the complexities of the principalship. You must develop and crystallize a vision of the principalship and how to build a learning community. This book provides the framework for your exploration of the principalship through the model by examining the various roles (Chapters 2–5) and processes (Chapters 6–11) for building a learning community within a school.

SUMMARY

The principalship is a dynamic, multidimensional, and demanding job in today's schools where a learning community must be created and nurtured. The constancy of change and continuous efforts to make schools better for all students, teachers, and the community provide opportunities for the principal to demonstrate various roles as described in this chapter through the Principalship Model. Keeping a clear focus on the roles and processes affecting the principalship will help a principal successfully build a learning community within the school.

REFLECTIVE ACTIVITIES

1. The Principal's Viewpoint

Interview two principals (elementary, middle, high, or private school) to inquire into the roles of the principalship. Interview one person who has three or fewer years of experience as a principal and another with five years or more so that you can compare different perspectives on the principalship. Using the content covered in this chapter, other readings, and your course work, prepare your questions before the interview. Be sure to ask both principals about their roles as described by the Principalship Model (educator, leader, manager, and inner person). Summarize the important points from the interviews and prepare to discuss them in class.

2. Stakeholder Viewpoints—Expectations About the Principal

Given the variety of stakeholders (teachers, staff, students, district office staff, superintendent, board of education, and community members), what do you believe are the stakeholders' expectations for the principalship? Pick at least one teacher and one staff member from the school site, one person from the district level, and one from the community to discuss their expectations for the principalship. Summarize the important points regarding stakeholders' expectations of the principal and prepare to discuss them in class.

3. A Principal's Work Day—Review/Shadow

Ask a principal to share a time log of a typical work day. Ask the principal to reflect on the roles or arrange to shadow the principal for a day. What insights did you gain in this review and discussion with the principal about the roles of the principalship? Summarize the important points and prepare to discuss them in class.

4. A Principal You Know

Select a principal you know, review the roles of the principal and processes for building a learning community with this person in mind, and then summarize the important points. Next, interview that principal and prepare to share the insights you gained in comparison to your initial review. Summarize your key insights and prepare to discuss them in class.

5. Your Perception of the Roles of the Principal—Principal's Reality

Write a brief description of the roles of the principal and why the principal exists as a part of the structure of the school. Are some roles more important than others? Discuss your written work and ideas with a principal. What insights and summarizing thoughts will you have to discuss in class?

SUGGESTED READINGS

Barth, Roland. 1990. *Improving Schools from Within*. San Francisco: Jossey-Bass.

Fullan, Michael G. 1988. *What's Worth Fighting For in the Principalship? Strategies for Taking Charge in the Elementary School Principalship*. Andover, MA: The Regional Laboratory for Educational Improvement of the Northeast and Islands.

Senge, Peter. 1990. *The Fifth Discipline: The Art and Practice of the Learning Organization*. New York: Doubleday.

Sergiovanni, Thomas J. 1996. *Leadership for the Schoolhouse: How Is It Different? Why Is It Important?* San Francisco: Jossey-Bass.

REFERENCES

Barth, Roland. 1990. *Improving Schools from Within*. San Francisco: Jossey-Bass.

Beck, Lynn G., and Joseph Murphy. 1996. *The Four Imperatives of a Successful School*. Thousand Oaks, CA: Corwin Press.

Boyer, Ernest L. 1995. *The Basic School: A Community for Learning*. Princeton, NJ: The Carnegie Foundation for the Advancement of Teaching.

Conley, David T. 1993. *Roadmap to Restructuring: Policies, Practices and the Emerging Visions of Schooling*. Eugene, OR: ERIC Clearinghouse on Educational Management, University of Oregon.

Cushman, Kathleen. 1992. Coalition of Essential Schools. *Horace* 9(1), 1–8.

Edmonds, Ronald. (1979) Effective Schools for the Urban Poor. *Educational Leadership* 37(12), 15–24.

Fullan, Michael G. 1988. *What's Worth Fighting For in the Principalship? Strategies for Taking Charge in the Elementary School Principalship*. Andover, MA: The Regional Laboratory for Educational Improvement of the Northeast and Islands.

Fullan, Michael G. 1993. *Change Forces: Probing the Depths of Educational Reform*. New York: The Falmer Press.

Glickman, Carl D. 1993. *Renewing America's Schools: A Guide for School-Based Action*. San Francisco: Jossey-Bass.

Goldman, Paul, Diane Dunlap, and David Conley. 1993. Facilitative Power and Non-Standardized Solutions to School Site Restructuring. *Educational Administration Quarterly* 92(1), 21–32.

Lambert, Linda, Deborah Walker, Diane P. Zimmerman, Joanne E. Cooper, Morgan Dale Lambert, Mary E. Gardner, and P. J. Ford Slack. 1995. *The Constructivist Leader*. New York: Teachers College Press.

Louis, Karen Seashore. 1992. *Restructuring and the Problem of Teachers' Work*. Chicago: The University of Chicago Press.

Meier, Deborah. 1995. *The Power of Their Ideas: Lessons for America from a Small School in Harlem*. Boston: Beacon Press.

Murphy, Joseph. 1994. Transformational Change and the Evolving Role of the Principalship: Early Empirical Evidence. In J. Murphy and K. S. Louis (Eds.), *Reshaping the Principalship: Insights from Transformational Reform Efforts*, 20–55. Thousand Oaks, CA: Corwin Press.

O'Neil, John. 1995. On Schools as Learning Organizations: A Conversation with Peter Senge. *Educational Leadership* 52(7), 20–23.

Peters, Tom, and Robert H. Waterman. 1981. *In Search of Excellence*. New York: Random House.

Prawat, Richard. 1992. From Individual Differences to Learning Communities—Our Changing Focus. *Educational Leadership* 49(7), 9–13.

Prawat, Richard. 1993. The Role of the Principal in the Development of Learning Communities. *Wingspan: The Pedamorphosis Communique* 9(2), 7–9.

Prestine, Nona. 1991. Completing the Essential Schools Metaphor: Principal as Enabler. Paper presented at the annual conference of the American Educational Research Association, Chicago.

Senge, Peter. 1990. *The Fifth Discipline: The Art and Practice of the Learning Organization*. New York: Doubleday.

Senge, Peter, Art Kliener, Charlotte Roberts, Richard B. Ross, and Bryan J. Smith. 1994. *The Fifth Discipline Fieldbook: Strategies and Tools for Building a Learning Organization*. New York: Doubleday.

Sergiovanni, Thomas J. 1994. *Building Community in Schools*. San Francisco: Jossey-Bass.

Sergiovanni, Thomas J. 1995. *The Principalship: A Reflective Practice Perspective*. 3d ed. Boston: Allyn and Bacon.

Sergiovanni, Thomas J. 1996. *Leadership for the Schoolhouse: How Is It Different? Why Is It Important?* San Francisco: Jossey-Bass.

Short, Paula M., and John T. Greer. 1997. *Leadership in Empowered Schools: Themes from Innovative Efforts*. Upper Saddle River, NJ: Merrill/Prentice Hall.

Sizer, Theodore. 1996. *Horace's Hope: What Works for the American High School*. Boston: Houghton Mifflin.

Smith, Stuart C., and Philip K. Piele, eds. 1996. *School Leadership: Handbook for Excellence*. 3d ed. Eugene, OR: ERIC Clearinghouse on Educational Management, University of Oregon.

Speck, Marsha. 1995. The Principalship for the Future—Today! *American Secondary Education* 23(4), 40–44.

PART I

ROLES OF THE PRINCIPAL IN BUILDING A LEARNING COMMUNITY

CHAPTER 2

PRINCIPAL AS EDUCATOR

PROBLEM SCENARIO

Now that you have been introduced to the Principalship Model, imagine yourself as the principal of a school where the learning community needs to see you in the role of educator. How do you see yourself carrying out the educator role on a daily basis within your school? Describe the role of the educator. What vital concepts and processes would you need in the role of principal as educator?

THE ROLE OF EDUCATOR

Building a learning community at a school is no easy task, but through the vital role of educator (Figure 2.1) the principal can facilitate a shared educational vision and focus. As an educator, the principal must be a continual learner who researches, studies programs and innovations, interacts and talks with others about educational issues, and models life-long learning with a clear focus on improving student and staff success. A learning community cannot exist unless the principal takes an active part as a learner and as one of the instructional leaders. Senge (O'Neil 1995) points out that a learning organization is one in which people at all levels collectively and continually enhance their capacity to create.

FIGURE 2.1
The Principal as
Educator

The Educator

- Learning and reflecting on practice
- Building and communicating the vision
- Reviewing research and exemplary programs
- Conducting and promoting collaborative research
- Understanding students and their needs
- Implementing and evaluating curriculum and instruction
- Improving school climate and culture
- Organizing and improving student services
- Monitoring students' progress

A leadership study by Bennis and Nanus (1985) found that successful leaders are perpetual learners. The study revealed that leaders learned how to learn in an organizational context. They constantly learned on the job and enabled and stimulated others to learn. In today's schools, principals must keep up-to-date to help the school continue to assess its actions and continue to grow and meet the diverse needs of students. Without continual learning and reinforcing the role of educator, a principal can quickly slide into incompetence. According to Fullan (1988), it is the principal exhibiting learning and professionalism in the role of educator that affects the professional culture.

LEARNING AND REFLECTING ON PRACTICE

As an educator and leader in the school, the principal must demonstrate being a lifelong learner. The principal must be the head learner in the school, demonstrating engagement in serious learning about what matters for the students' education and the learning community (teachers, staff, and parents). As Barth (1990) states:

> The principal need no longer be the "headmaster" or "instructional leader," pretending to know all. . . . The more crucial role of the principal is as head learner, engaging in the most important enterprise of the schoolhouse—experiencing, displaying, modeling,

and celebrating what it is hoped and expected that teachers and pupils will do.[1]

The principal's commitment to continuous learning is the most important aspect in creating a school's learning environment. Without adults (principal, teachers, and staff) who are committed to continuous inquiry and learning, a school will not create the environment for learning for students. In a learning community, adults and students alike learn and each member energizes and contributes to the learning of the others (Barth 1990, 46). The principal is the central agent in creating a successful learning community. The school must be a community of learners with the principal demonstrating continuous learning.

Barth (1990) comments on what a school should be:

> [It is] . . . the concept of the school as a community of learners, a place where all participants—teachers, principals, parents, and students—engage in learning and teaching. School is not a place for important people who do not need to learn and unimportant people who do. Instead, school is a place where students discover, and adults rediscover, the joys, the difficulties, and the satisfactions of learning. . . . In a community of learners, adults and children learn simultaneously and in the same place to think critically and analytically and to solve problems that are important to them. In a community of learners, learning is endemic and mutually visible.[2]

Thus a crucial question for a principal viewing the daily interactions within the school is whether there is a mutually visible community of learners. Beck and Murphy (1996) found that the learning imperative is the organizing center for a successful school.

> A successful school has . . . a strong and passionate commitment to an expansive notion of learning—one that emphasizes problem solving, research, creativity, technology, collaborative work, broad conceptions of literacy, and communication. (p. 58)

A principal as educator and learner cannot accept the status quo, but is committed to continual growth, problem-solving, and broadening the notions of learning within the school. A principal must be a reflective practitioner who is capable of continuous learning and reflecting on practice as opportunities for leadership and modeling occur throughout the school day. Reflective practice allows a principal

---

[1] Reprinted with permission of Jossey-Bass Inc. from *Improving Schools from Within*, 46, by Roland Barth. © 1990 by Jossey-Bass Inc., Publishers.

[2] Ibid, 43.

to use professional knowledge as a way of thinking about, reflecting on, deciding about, and acting on practices. According to Schon (1983) a reflective practitioner tries to make sense of actions by reflecting on the understandings implicit in an action and embodying these reflective thoughts in further action.

Sergiovanni (1995) in *The Principalship: A Reflective Practice Perspective* reinforces the importance of reflective practice for the principalship:

> Reflective practice requires that principals have a healthy respect for, be well informed about, and use the best available theory and research and accumulated practice wisdom. All these sources of information help increase understanding and inform practice. (p. 36)

What makes a difference for all learners is the ability of principals to raise questions, examine the school environment, clarify issues, stimulate thought and learning, encourage reflective practice on the part of the staff as well as themselves, and carry on a daily dialogue about what types of learning experiences and environments are conducive to a learning community.

Learning about schooling and the work of the principalship is an ongoing process as the principal integrates various perspectives, research, ideas, values, and practices to improve learning at the school. As a learner, the principal should be continuously invigorated both professionally and personally by new ideas and insights. As a learning leader, the principal certainly makes the difference for an effective school and success for all students. The passion for learning and the support generated by the learning will provide the principal with the energy to continue working for the success of all students (Beck and Murphy 1996).

Goldring and Rallis (1993) in *Principals of Dynamic Schools* explains the vital learner role the principal plays:

> The principal serves as a role model, establishing an atmosphere in which all members of the school's organization work to improve the processes and outcomes. In this way, the principal encourages a self-correcting school. (p. 140)

Patterson (1993) emphasizes the importance of the principal serving as a role model for learning and creating reflective practices within a school in *Leadership for Tomorrow's Schools*:

> Leaders need to nurture a reflective environment, one characterized by people suspending premature judgments, making themselves vulnerable through questioning their own and others' thinking, and

committing themselves as a group to the belief that through reflective thought *we* indeed will prove to be smarter than *me*.[3]

The use of reflective practice is a part of creating a learning community where each person's thoughts and actions are valued. Senge (O'Neil 1995) states that creating a reflective environment and a degree of safety where individuals can rediscover what they really care about is an important step in the process. Bringing people together in this way allows their individual visions to emerge, from which they can begin creating a new shared vision.

Senge (O'Neil 1995) clarifies the importance of learning and reflection within a school:

> We communicate our individual visions to one another and eventually start to create a field of shared meaning—where there really is a deep level of trust and mutual understanding—and we gradually begin to build a shared vision. Actually having shared visions exist is so profoundly different from writing a vision statement. . . . It takes a long time, and it's a process that involves a lot of reflection and a great deal of listening and mutual understanding. (p. 22)

The principal as a reflective practitioner develops and nurtures a process and environment for the learning community to interact, create and sustain a vision, implement goals, and evaluate outcomes. As a learner, the principal must develop an ongoing capacity to help the learning community continually grow and meet the learning needs of students and staff.

BUILDING AND COMMUNICATING THE VISION

Discussions of the vital role of vision appear in almost every book on educational and organizational excellence (Fullan 1988). Bennis and Nanus (1985) found that compelling vision is the key quality in heads of highly successful organizations.

> All of the leaders to who [sic] we spoke seemed to have been masters at selecting, synthesizing, and articulating an appropriate vision of the future. . . . If there is a spark of genius in the leadership function

---

[3] Reprinted with permission of Association for Supervision and Curriculum Development from *Leadership for Tomorrow's Schools,* 11, by Jerry L. Patterson. © 1993 by Association for Supervision and Curriculum Development.

at all, it must lie in this transcending ability, a kind of magic, to assemble—out of all the variety of images, signals, forecasts, and alternatives—a clear, articulated vision of the future that is at once single, easily understood, clearly desirable, and energizing.[4]

Vision-building for the principal, then, is very much an interactive process and depends heavily on two-way communication skills, empathy, and exposure to a variety of ideas and stimuli (Fullan 1988). Sergiovanni (1995) sees vision as the ability to create and communicate a view of a desired state of affairs that induces commitment among those working in the organization. Vision is the essence of what the school communicates in a holistic way through words, actions, and written material about what the school stands for and hopes for the future. The principal as educator must not only have a vision, but also facilitate, translate, and build it into a school community vision for educating students. The principal's vision for schooling must move from "mine" to "our" to build commitment to a shared, preferred future.

Kouzes and Posner (1995) found in their leadership study that successful leaders define a common purpose and then effectively communicate a vision so that others come to share the vision as their own.

> It is a process of engaging constituents in conversations about their lives, about their hopes and dreams. Remember that leadership is a dialogue, not a monologue. Leadership isn't about imposing the leader's solo dream; it's about developing a *shared* sense of destiny. It's about enrolling others so that they can see how their own interests and aspirations are aligned with the vision and can thereby become mobilized to commit their individual energies to its realization. A vision is *inclusive* of the constituents' aspirations; it's an ideal and unique image of the future for the *common* good.[5]

Without the principal's vigilance and daily actions as a builder of the vision, the school will not be successful. A school that lacks vision does not have a clear focus for learning. Articulating the school vision forces the principal and school to hold themselves accountable for acting in a way that is congruent with the vision. The vision states how the school wants to work with students and other members of the school learning community. Block (1987) states it clearly:

---

[4] Reprinted with permission of HarperCollins Publishers from *Leaders: The Strategies for Taking Charge,* 101, by Warren Bennis and Burt Nanus. © 1985 by HarperCollins Publishers.

[5] Reprinted with permission of Jossey-Bass Inc. from *The Leadership Challenge: How to Keep Getting Extraordinary Things Done in Organizations,* 124, by James M. Kouzes and Barry Z. Posner. © 1995 by Jossey-Bass Inc., Publishers.

Once we have created a vision and communicated it to the people around us, it becomes a benchmark for evaluating all of our actions. (p. 105)

Expectations for the principal as a visionary and a builder of vision can be seen in numerous principalship job advertisements, such as this example from a California school district:

> **Visionary abilities:** Is positive, innovative, creative, and able to articulate vision and provide focus for others; uses talent to transform vision into reality; and has the ability to deal with changing district.

Sergiovanni in *Moral Leadership* (1992) says:

Vision informs our work . . . as we need leaders who understand how children and adults learn, and keep on learning . . . [and] who understand how to build communities of learners. (p. 1)

A vision must clearly focus on core beliefs, and the principal must express the vision daily in words and actions. Remember the words of Ralph Waldo Emerson (Seldes 1983):

What you do speaks so loudly that no one can hear what you say. (p. 238)

REFLECTIONS: AS A PRINCIPAL, WHAT WOULD BE YOUR VISION

FOR A SCHOOL? HOW WOULD YOU BUILD A SCHOOL VISION?

TAKE THE TIME NOW TO WRITE DOWN ELEMENTS OF YOUR VISION.

The principal must provide the leadership and learning environment necessary to bring the vision of the school to fruition. Senge (O'Neil 1995) states that principals with the greatest impact tend to see their job as creating an environment where teachers can continually learn, discuss, and develop new ideas and teaching strategies. As the leader of the school, the principal helps translate vision into the reality of school life. The principal is ultimately held accountable for how the school vision is carried out. The principal's actions speak to the overall beliefs and expectations held for the school. In leading the school, the principal clarifies the current school status and gains the school community's commitment to the future. Rarely does a successful school exist without an effective principal (Sergiovanni 1995, 14; Edmonds, 1979). The principal demonstrates leadership in the ability to cause change and build direction through effective interaction with the learning community. The collaborative process of building and communicating a learning community vision will be discussed in Chapter 6.

REVIEWING RESEARCH AND EXEMPLARY PROGRAMS

For a principal, reviewing research and exemplary programs becomes an important habit of mind and reflective process. Research offers insight into which educational programs work and why. Too often principals jump on the bandwagon of a new education program before investigating its track record through research. Visitations and reviews of exemplary programs give the principal an opportunity to work with fellow staff members in a research and review process. Through analysis of the various aspects of exemplary programs, the principal and school can decide if there is a place for a new program in their learning community. The act of reviewing research and exemplary programs reveals an aspect of the educator role of the principalship as a learner and researcher.

CONDUCTING AND PROMOTING COLLABORATIVE RESEARCH

In providing leadership and improving learning within a school, the principal needs to conduct and promote collaborative research. This type of research involves studying, learning, and applying techniques that focus on improving student learning. The principal, with the help of the rest of the learning community, can assess the status of the school through the use of a collaborative research model, as described by Sagor (1992). Collaborative research (Figure 2.2) includes formulating the problem, collecting data, analyzing the data, reporting the results, and planning for action that will improve learning within the school and involve members of the learning community in the process. The use of Sagor's collaborative research process is an important tool for overcoming problems in schools. Collaborative research is conducted by people who want to do something to improve their own situation. It is a means by which individuals at a school can improve the

FIGURE 2.2

Collaborative
Research Process

Adapted from Sagor
1992.

1. Problem Formulation

2. Data Collection

3. Data Analysis

4. Reporting of Results

5. Action Planning

learning process and contribute to the education profession. Thus, the principal, in using these techniques, demonstrates the ability to deal with problems with a clear process that combines learning, use of research, and planning. Sagor (1992) explains the collaborative research process:

> Collaborative action research is a process that enables teachers to improve the teaching-learning process while also contributing to the development of their own profession.[6]

Goldring and Rallis (1993) emphasize the importance of the principal's role as a collaborative researcher:

> As inquirer, the principal takes charge of an evaluation-minded school, modeling behaviors that encourage the asking of questions and the use of systematically collected data. In this role of inquirer, the principal leads the process of collaborative problem solving and shared decision making. (p. 139)

The principal and others in the learning community can use collaborative research as a tool for continual improvement. The intent of this book is simply to introduce this technique as a vital tool for a learning community. School learning communities need to use research, formulate problems, collect and analyze data, report results, and plan actions continually. Collaborative research becomes part of a learning community's daily operations, not imposed from outside but carried on by professionals within the schools based on specific issues and needs. It fosters a continuous mode of inquiry and reflection that should be the norm within a learning community.

Sagor (1992) summarizes the key points for collaborative research that are important for a principal and learning community:

---

[6] Reprinted with permission of Association for Supervision and Curriculum Development from *How to Conduct Collaborative Action Research* (ASCD #611-93011), 6, by Richard Sagor. © 1992 by Association for Supervision and Curriculum Development.

> *Action* research . . . is conducted by people who want to do something to improve their own situation. . . . Action researchers undertake a study because they want to know whether they can do something in a better way.[7]

> Research is defined . . . as any effort toward disciplined inquiry. Many of us have been schooled in the notion that only investigations that can be reduced to numbers qualify as research. . . . Action research involves a wide array of methods derived from both the quantitative and qualitative domains. In the collaborative action research process, the focus of the research is defined by the practitioners themselves.[8]

> By turning to *collaborative* action research, however, we can renew our commitment to thoughtful teaching and also begin developing an active community of professionals.[9]

Thus, collaborative research involves a working learning process and the creation of a culture that values engaging in research and learning for the improvement of student learning and the school. Members of the learning community conduct research through a collaborative process within the school rather than always relying on outside research sources.

UNDERSTANDING STUDENTS AND THEIR NEEDS

The principal as educator must understand the characteristics and needs of students through careful investigation with the rest of the community to better align the curriculum, instruction, and assessment based on the students' needs. Creating a clear understanding of students and their learning needs enables the principal and teachers to be more precise in providing appropriate curriculum, instruction, and assessment procedures. Too often, schools and principals fail to understand the students' needs and merely adopt curriculum, instructional, and assessment practices that are a mismatch for what the students really need to be successful. Combining collaborative research with the need to understand specific student characteristics and needs will provide a thoughtful process for the alignment of curriculum, instruction, and assessment procedures within a learning community.

[7] Ibid, 7.
[8] Ibid, 9.
[9] Ibid, 10.

IMPLEMENTING AND EVALUATING CURRICULUM AND INSTRUCTION

As educator, the principal must help develop, align, implement, and evaluate curriculum and instruction. Being an educator distinguishes a principal's role from that of other leadership positions because the importance of understanding and experiencing teaching (instruction), content (curriculum), and assessing outcomes (assessment) provides a base of knowledge for understanding schooling. By working with teachers, students, staff, and parents to develop, align, implement, and evaluate curriculum and instruction, the principal gains the advantage of knowing what goes on in the classroom and what kind of overall education students are receiving. In the educator role, the principal must have a deep understanding of instructional practices, curriculum content, and assessment means. Further discussion of these topics will take place in Chapter 7.

IMPROVING SCHOOL CLIMATE AND CULTURE

The school culture is another important factor in creating a learning community and as part of the educator role of the principalship. The principal must be a climate- and culture-creator who deals with the complex atmosphere of a campus, ranging from safety and discipline issues to interactions among students, teachers, parents, and staff. According to Saphier and King (1985), the essential elements for a principal to foster in creating an effective culture are collegiality, trust and confidence, caring, celebration and humor, tangible support, high expectations, experimentation, appreciation and recognition, involvement in decision making, protection of what is important, traditions, and communication that is honest and open. This book will elaborate on creating climate and culture in Chapters 3 and 6.

ORGANIZING AND IMPROVING STUDENT SERVICES

Student success is the key focus for the principal. As an educator the principal must organize and improve student services. Through collaborative efforts within and without the school, the principal and other stakeholders of the school must identify vital student services and how to improve them. Today's principal must look at not only attendance, counseling, and student activities, but also technology, nutrition and health, and career opportunities. Student services within a school make a variety of educational opportunities available to students. As an educator with the knowledge of teaching, curriculum, and assessment, the principal must ensure that student services are meeting the needs of students who must be ready for the twenty-first century. The principal must work through the important issues of organizing, reviewing, improving, or eliminating student services as needed to build a successful school.

MONITORING STUDENTS' PROGRESS

Assessing student progress is a major focus of the principal as educator. How does the principal evaluate student progress? Educators, including the principal, must look at hard data to see how students are progressing. They must closely monitor student progress to keep track of such issues as reading ability and literacy and avoid shuffling students off to the next grade without the skills and abilities they need to succeed. The educator role requires the principal to understand how to use various types of assessment. Assessment should inform the practices of the teachers and the school as a whole. Chapter 7 deals with assessment in an expanded discussion of the importance of monitoring student progress.

AN EXAMPLE OF A PRINCIPAL'S EDUCATOR ROLE

This chapter has introduced the principal's educator role. What does that role look like in the daily life of a principal? The principal's interactions and reflections with teachers, staff, students, parents, and the community help define the educator role. Daily issues of schooling arise that get to the heart of the school's vision. The principal tackles problems by identifying the issues and setting a process for teachers and others to study, learn, and reflect on how to resolve a problem.

For example, suppose a school has many students who read poorly. As an educator, Juanita, the principal of Cesar Chavez Elementary, must help the faculty define the reading achievement problem and decide what actions might increase reading achievement. Juanita facilitates and guides the improvement of the school reading program by collaborating with teachers, engaging them in dialogue, study, classroom visits, and research on exemplary reading programs. Juanita and the teachers might decide to realign or implement specific reading curriculum and instruction programs that better meet students' reading needs. These decisions will be made only after Juanita and the teachers have spent considerable time collecting data in classrooms and studying various reading programs. This process enables Juanita to help bring about collective learning on the issues of reading improvement. Continuous monitoring of student reading progress helps keep the focus on the issue of improving student reading achievement. As principal, Juanita cultivates a collaborative spirit within the school through constant focus on working together as a school learning community—not as isolated individuals—to address reading achievement. Parents and other members of the community need to be aware of the issues of reading achievement, and Juanita as principal must provide information on an ongoing basis to help inform them about the progress and changes being made to improve student reading achievement. These forms of communication include family reading nights, gift of reading programs where students take home books to share with the family, and a newsletter discussing student achievement. Finally, as principal, Juanita continues to study, learn, and reflect on the reading practices within the school, thus communicating a clear, consistent educational focus. Juanita's teachers and community know where the school stands on reading achievement for all students.

SUMMARY

To build a learning community within a school, the principal must carry out the educator role by being a continual learner. Collaboratively developing the climate and culture within a learning community causes the principal to be a vision-builder, moving from "my" vision to "our" vision. Understanding students' characteristics and needs aligned with curriculum, instruction, and assessment is a key job of the principal as educator. A principal must have a deep understanding as an educator and a thirst for continual learning. These characteristics will help the principal create a true learning community where all can see that learning is thriving on a daily basis and the actions of all members demonstrate the importance of learning.

REFLECTIVE ACTIVITIES

1. The Principal as Educator

At the beginning of this chapter, you were asked to think about the educator role of the principal. After reading this chapter, how do you see yourself as a principal carrying out the role of the educator within your school? Describe the educator role with your own personal examples. What vital concepts and processes does a principal as educator need to implement?

2. The Principal as Learner

How do you envision the principal as a learner? If you were a principal, how would you act in the role of principal as learner? How would the various stakeholders understand your role as a learner?

3. Aspects of the Educator Role

After reading this chapter, what aspects of the educator's role would you like to explore more: builder of the vision; learner; collaborative researcher; understanding student characteristics and needs; alignment of curriculum, instruction, and assessment; climate- and culture-creator? Choose two aspects to explore. How will you gather data and information on these aspects of the principalship? Be prepared to discuss your findings.

4. A Principal's View of the Educator Role

Interview a principal about each aspect of the educator role of the principalship. What insights did you gain on the various aspects of the educator role? Be prepared to discuss your insights in class or in writing.

SUGGESTED READINGS

Barth, Roland. 1990. *Improving Schools from Within*. San Francisco: Jossey-Bass.

Kouzes, James M., and Barry Z. Posner. 1995. *The Leadership Challenge: How to Keep Getting Extraordinary Things Done in Organizations*. San Francisco: Jossey-Bass.

O'Neil, John. 1995. On Schools as Learning Organizations: A Conversation with Peter Senge. *Educational Leadership* 52(7), 20–23.

Patterson, Jerry L. 1993. *Leadership for Tomorrow's Schools*. Alexandria, VA: Association for Supervision and Curriculum Development.

Sagor, Richard. 1992. *How to Conduct Collaborative Action Research*. Alexandria, VA: Association for Supervision and Curriculum Development.

Sergiovanni, Thomas J. 1995. *The Principalship: A Reflective Practice Perspective*. 3d ed. Boston: Allyn and Bacon.

REFERENCES

Barth, Roland. 1990. *Improving Schools from Within*. San Francisco: Jossey-Bass.

Beck, Lynn G., and Joseph Murphy. 1996. *The Four Imperatives of a Successful School*. Thousand Oaks, CA: Corwin Press.

Bennis, Warren, and Burt Nanus. 1985. *Leaders: The Strategies for Taking Charge*. New York: Harper and Row.

Block, Peter. 1987. *The Empowered Manager*. San Francisco: Jossey-Bass.

Edmonds, Ronald. 1979. *A Discussion of the Literature and Issues Related to Effective Schooling*. 49 pages. ED 170 394.

Fullan, Michael G. 1988. *What's Worth Fighting For in the Principalship? Strategies for Taking Charge in the Elementary School Principalship*. Andover, MA: The Regional Laboratory for Educational Improvement of the Northeast and Islands.

Goldring, Ellen B., and Sharon F. Rallis. 1993. *Principals of Dynamic Schools: Taking Charge of Change*. Newbury Park, CA: Corwin Press.

Kouzes, James M., and Barry Z. Posner. 1995. *The Leadership Challenge: How to Keep Getting Extraordinary Things Done in Organizations*. San Francisco: Jossey-Bass.

O'Neil, John. 1995. On Schools as Learning Organizations: A Conversation with Peter Senge. *Educational Leadership* 52(7), 20–23.

Patterson, Jerry L. 1993. *Leadership for Tomorrow's Schools*. Alexandria, VA: Association for Supervision and Curriculum Development.

Sagor, Richard. 1992. *How to Conduct Collaborative Action Research.* Alexandria, VA: Association for Supervision and Curriculum Development.

Saphier, Jon, and Matthew King. March 1985. Good Seeds Grow in Strong Cultures. *Educational Leadership* 42(6): 67–74.

Schon, Donald. 1983. *The Reflective Practitioner: How Professionals Think in Action.* New York: Basic Books.

Seldes, George. 1983. *The Great Quotations.* Secaucus, NJ: Citadel Press.

Sergiovanni, Thomas J. 1992. *Moral Leadership: Getting to the Heart of School Improvement.* San Francisco: Jossey-Bass.

Sergiovanni, Thomas J. 1995. *The Principalship: A Reflective Practice Perspective.* 3d ed. Boston: Allyn and Bacon.

CHAPTER 3

PRINCIPAL AS LEADER

The Role of the Leader

Leadership for a Learning Community

Appraising the Present and Envisioning the Future

Communicating the Vision

Determining Capacity for Change and Planning and Implementing Change

Deploying Self

Empowering Staff and Community

Building Trust

Monitoring and Assessing Progress

Showing Appreciation and Celebrating Accomplishments

Taking Care of Staff, Students, and Community

Motivating All People in the School Community

Using Human Skills (Interpersonal and Group)

PROBLEM SCENARIO

As newly appointed principal of Hope School, you are expected to provide leadership to the school learning community. How do you see your leadership role? After working with and observing you for the first month, how would others in the community—teachers, staff, students, parents—describe your leadership? As a principal, what aspects of the leadership role do you believe are important for students as well as overall school success?

THE ROLE OF THE LEADER

The leader role of the principal (see Figure 3.1) is pivotal because it involves putting the beliefs of the principal as educator into action to achieve student and school success. As a leader, a principal must be able to appraise the present, anticipate the future, and collaborate with the school's stakeholders to develop a school vision that will yield a learning experience for all members of the learning community. The

FIGURE 3.1

The Principal as
Leader

Leader Role

- Appraising the present
- Envisioning the future
- Communicating the vision
- Determining capacity for change
- Planning and implementing change
- Deploying self
- Empowering staff and community
- Building trust
- Monitoring and assessing progress
- Showing appreciation and celebrating accomplishments
- Taking care of staff, students, and community
- Motivating members of the school community
- Using human skills (interpersonal and group)

leadership role of the principal helps determine the capacity for change, including assessing individual and group capacities for change.

The leader role requires the principal to select and practice effective leadership styles and focus on school improvement. Empowering staff and students, building trust, monitoring and assessing progress, and providing assistance are critical elements of the leader role. As a leader, the principal must show appreciation and celebrate accomplishments as the learning community changes. Taking care of the students, staff, and the community should become a clear emphasis for the principal. Motivating a variety of people is an important part of the leader role where the principal must employ many leadership skills, for both interpersonal and group interaction. This chapter will explore the leader role of the principalship as a part of developing a learning community, including a discussion of what leadership means for the principalship in theory and practice. The reader will gain a clear picture of how leadership greatly improves the education of students.

Throughout the day-to-day experiences of life in the school, the principal must understand the critical importance of the leadership role. The principal's leadership satisfies and nurtures the ongoing need for developing a learning community within the school for every student. Key components of the principal's leadership role are regularly encouraging and empowering staff members to take responsibility for nourishing the spirit of inquiry that fosters continual learning. This role is crucial in establishing and nurturing a learning community.

LEADERSHIP FOR A LEARNING COMMUNITY

"Leadership" is a word on everyone's lips. The young attack it and the old grow wistful for it. Parents have lost it and police seek it. Experts claim it and artists spurn it, while scholars want it. Philosophers reconcile it (as authority) with liberty and theologians demonstrate its compatibility with conscience. If bureaucrats pretend they have it, politicians wish they did. Everybody agrees there is less of it than there used to be.[1]

Many authors have contributed to the body of knowledge on leadership, offering a variety of definitions of the term (Bennis and Nanus 1985; Kouzes and Posner 1995; Sergiovanni 1995). Leadership has been an elusive concept, and numerous research studies have shown no consensus on the topic. Let's explore the concept of leadership within a school learning community.

REFLECTIONS: HOW DOES THIS LEADERSHIP KNOWLEDGE BASE

APPLY TO THE PRINCIPALSHIP AND BUILDING A LEARNING COM-

MUNITY? WHAT IS THE LEADERSHIP ROLE OF A PRINCIPAL

WITHIN A SCHOOL LEARNING COMMUNITY? TAKE THE TIME TO

WRITE DOWN YOUR THOUGHTS.

This chapter will provide an overview of the leadership role and its application to the principalship and a school learning community. A school needs leadership from the principal that will allow it to evolve into a true learning community. Through the principal's leadership, a learning community will be able to deal with the problems and opportunities of today and invest in its capacity to embrace tomorrow, because all members remain focused on enhancing and expanding their collective awareness and capabilities. The principal, through leadership, must foster an organization that can itself learn and that helps each member of the learning community to be a lifelong learner on a never-ending development path. The principal as leader must help construct and nurture a learning environment where members can

---

[1] Reprinted with permission of HarperCollins Publishers from *Leaders: The Strategies for Taking Charge*, 198, by Warren Bennis and Burt Nanus. © 1985 by HarperCollins Publishers.

hold and seek a vision, reflect and inquire, build collective capabilities, and understand systems to improve learning for all students. Senge et al. (1994) state:

> Encouraging *learning* is the *primary task of leadership,* and perhaps the only way that a leader can genuinely influence or inspire others.[2]

Through the process of learning, a principal as leader engages the diverse members of the school community in continual improvement and increases the likelihood of success for all. This discovery of ideas and solutions emerges from learning together and can transform a school. The principal must use the leadership role to promote continuous learning together, thus developing and inspiring new ideas and solutions to existing and emerging problems.

APPRAISING THE PRESENT AND ENVISIONING THE FUTURE

The principal as leader, along with other members of the learning community, continues to appraise the status of the school through an inquiry mode. The leader must engage others in the learning community in analyzing its current status and how it fits with visions for the present and future. Constant dialogue and interaction among members of the learning community allow appraising, learning, envisioning, and acting to take place. The Learning Loop (see Figure 3.2) illustrates the interaction and dialogue that must occur constantly to inform practices within the learning community.

The leader must communicate through words and actions the analysis of the present and the development of the shared vision on a daily basis. The leader learns to expand current knowledge and understanding for the improvement of the school as well as to encourage all learning community members to develop a shared vision of the school. Senge et al. (1994) defined a shared vision as the core of a learning organization:

> Shared Vision—building a sense of commitment in a group, by developing shared images of the future we seek to create, and the principles and guiding practices by which we hope to get there.[3]

---

[2] Reprinted with permission of Doubleday from *The Fifth Discipline Fieldbook: Strategies and Tools for Building a Learning Organization*, 65, by Peter Senge, Art Kliener, Charlotte Roberts, Richard B. Ross, and Bryan J. Smith. © 1994 by Doubleday.
[3] Ibid, 6.

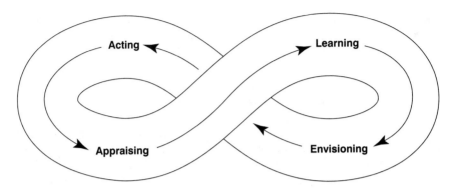

FIGURE 3.2
Learning Loop

In Chapter 6 the reader will learn about creating a vision statement and carrying out and communicating that vision through collaboration. The principal as leader has an important part in making a difference for the school now and in the future. According to Senge et al. (1994), the core of a learning organization's work is based on personal mastery and mental models that fit with what a principal as leader must do within the school.

> The core of learning organization work is based upon . . . "learning disciplines"—lifelong programs of study and practice:
>
> ▪ Personal mastery—learning to expand our personal capacity to create the results we most desire, and creating an organizational environment which encourages all its members to develop themselves toward the goals and purposes they choose.
>
> ▪ Mental models—reflecting upon, continually clarifying, and improving our internal pictures of the world, and seeing how they shape our actions and decisions.[4]

The principal as leader must find ways to continue to learn, keep up-to-date, and then collaborate with others in the school to apply ideas and innovations to help the entire learning community improve. The learning, reflecting, and clarifying activities of the principal as leader will demonstrate practices that must become the norm in a learning community. The principal as leader must engage in the vital processes of creating and reflecting on mental models of what a school should be and reviewing the current status and the envisioned future. The dialogues

[4] Ibid, 6.

and creation of new models shape actions and decisions for creating the school as envisioned to foster learning for all. Too often the principal is drowning in daily duties and has little time to give to appraising the present status and envisioning the future of the school. The principal and other members of the learning community should be able to look forward to creating, instead of merely reacting to issues. The emerging models provide the school learning community with opportunities.

The principal as a leader must have a means to reflect on practice. The Principal's Reflective Practice Model (see Figure 3.3) depicts the elements of engaging in reflective practice. The initial influences on a principal's practice come from learned skills developed from studying research, theory, related knowledge, experience, and observing exemplary practice. Building on the initial level of influence, principals can receive support, mentoring, and coaching to help influence their practice and success. A principal's values, intuition, and imagination influence practice and must be considered. As principals examine their practices, each of these elements helps in the reflective process to confirm a current practice or develop a change in practice. How would

Sources for Reflective Practice

FIGURE 3.3
Principal's Reflective Practice Model

you see yourself as a principal using this model to analyze and improve on your practices as a principal?

Reflective practice is an important source of continuous learning for the principal and serves as a model of learning and growth for the entire learning community. Reflecting on practice allows the principal to develop an important habit of mind that involves appraising the present and assessing practices for the future. A continuous learning process with reflection thus becomes routine for the school and the principal. The principal and other members of the learning community can check the envisioned future with the school's present practices and make decisions about future practices.

COMMUNICATING THE VISION

As the school develops its vision and models on the path toward becoming a learning community, the principal's role as leader is to help facilitate and communicate the vision on an ongoing basis within the school and to the larger community.

The leader is the vision-keeper, as Lashway (1996) expresses in the following statement:

> The leader embodies the vision in thought, word, and deed. Visionaries do not just communicate their dreams in so many words, says Gardner; "they convey their stories by the kinds of lives they themselves lead and, through example, seek to inspire in their followers." Clearly, leaders remain the key people in the process even if they are not the sole authors of the vision. (p. 135)

A vision that is not clearly articulated is one that is likely to be lost. As the promise and original excitement of the vision wane, the waves of daily tasks can dampen or drown the enthusiasm and spirit for the vision. A written statement or compact clearly stating the vision of the school helps keep the vision real, as Chapter 6 will show. Communicating the vision again and again—and again, if needed—is a key role of the principal as leader. Barth (1990) comments on the importance of communicating the vision:

> Teachers and principals who convey their craft knowledge and their visions to other adults derive enormous personal satisfaction and recognition. Vision unlocked is energy unlocked.[5]

---

[5] Reprinted with permission of Jossey-Bass Inc. from *Improving Schools from Within*, 151, by Roland Barth. © 1990 by Jossey-Bass Inc., Publishers.

Too often visions are created in schools, but then left to dissipate into obscurity. It is important for the principal and learning community to implement and communicate their vision to prevent outside forces—a district office, state department, or national commission—from imposing their prescriptions on the school. Visions originating from outside the school have never really worked. When members of a school community create and communicate their own vision, it becomes more of a reality for all as they participate in its development and refinement.

DETERMINING CAPACITY FOR CHANGE AND PLANNING AND IMPLEMENTING CHANGE

The principal in the role of leader must determine the learning community's capacity for change and then foster the change process through planning and implementing change within the school. After studying, discussing, researching, analyzing, experimenting, and learning with other members of the learning community, the principal is able to determine the capacity for change. A learning community, with the principal, can foster the capacity for change by taking note of the comments of Senge et al. (1994):

> If there is one single thing a learning organization does well, it is helping people embrace change. People in learning organizations react more quickly when their environment changes because they know how to anticipate changes that are going to occur (which is different [from] trying to predict the future), and how to create the kinds of changes they want. Change and learning may not exactly be synonymous, but they are inextricably linked.[6]

The principal must foster learning within the school so that learning becomes the basis for change. A school learning community must engage in a constant learning dialogue that helps anticipate, create, and implement meaningful programs to meet the needs of its students. Change does not occur for its own sake but results from careful reflection on the learning community's practices and on what changes will improve learning for all. The principal is the chief engineer of sustain-

[6] Reprinted with permission of Doubleday from *The Fifth Discipline Fieldbook: Strategies and Tools for Building a Learning Organization*, 11, by Peter Senge et al. © 1994 by Doubleday.

ing the capacity for change through daily actions of promoting learning that analyzes the present, reviews research and practices, uses action research, and makes recommendations collaboratively to implement new ideas that fit the unique needs of the school. The principal's actions can foster the school's continual capacity for change by encouraging involvement in and learning about new ideas and programs. Continuous learning and examining current practices are intertwined with change to achieve the vision of the school learning community.

DEPLOYING SELF

Deploying self as a principal and leader means getting out of the office and interacting with others. It is a key to carrying out the vision and the daily efforts at the school. Teachers and students need to have daily contact with the principal to hear concerns, receive information, share joys, and see learning taking place. It is the ability to be visible, talk, observe, assist, listen, and learn that allow the principal to be in constant contact with a variety of constituents. Leadership involves being there when people need your help and guidance as well as when they need affirmation of their work. Principals who deploy themselves know the importance of getting out of the office and making contact. Oftentimes the principal can allay a person's concerns about issues at the school simply by being out and about. Being visible and deploying oneself helps create a community within the school. As stakeholders see the principal regularly and in a variety of ways—helping teachers, working with students, learning together, talking to parents and community members, and solving problems—they develop a sense of commitment to the work of the learning community.

EMPOWERING STAFF
AND COMMUNITY

Leaders know that they gain strength from having a variety of followers and supporters to help them build a vision. An important lesson for a principal is how to empower the staff and the whole community to help carry out the school vision. Leaders do not do things alone, and thus the principal can do much more through the empowerment of teachers, staff, students, parents, and the rest of the community (Short and Greer 1997). Once clear goals and the vision are established, the principal must allow and help others within the school community to take ownership and develop the means to carry out the goals. The principal is only as strong as the school community that works toward and supports the school vision and goals. By empowering the staff, the principal can get more accomplished and develop ownership and pride in their work together as they build their learning community. Too often principals try to do things alone and fail to build ownership into the school efforts. By empowering others the principal helps build the sense of commitment and ownership necessary to carry out their joint efforts for improving the school.

BUILDING TRUST

Trust building is an important beginning task for any new principal, as is keeping that trust once it exists. Trust building is neither an easy nor a quick task for a principal. Trust develops over time based on working relationships within and outside the school. Teachers, staff, and students see trust develop as their daily working relationships unfold with the principal. The principal's commitment to action, developing relationships, and follow-through helps build a foundation for trust. Trust is a key ingredient to develop a learning community where each person feels free to express ideas, take actions, and evaluate outcomes in an atmosphere where there is no retaliation or ill feelings by the principal. Without trust, the learning community cannot function. Trust is a key element of a learning community's soul. Without this important level of trust, individuals will not fully participate or commit to the work of the learning community. A principal must always remember the importance of trust. Once the learning community loses trust in the principal, it is very difficult, if not impossible, to regain.

MONITORING AND ASSESSING PROGRESS

Another important focus for the principal as leader is to monitor and assess the community's efforts to change and its progress toward goals. If schools are to be successful, then principals working with the school community must monitor and assess the progress of student achievement and the overall achievement of the school.

Schmoker (1996) in *Results: The Key to Continuous School Improvement*, offers insight into the importance of the principal's leadership in school improvement and the need for monitoring progress:

The kind of significant, sustained improvement that we need in schools will not occur in an isolated, free-lance culture, where no one knows what anyone else is doing or what each other's operative goals are. That is a system in disarray.

Schools improve when purpose and effort unite. One key is leadership that recognizes its most vital function: to keep everyone's eyes on the prize of improved student learning. The crush of competing agendas and distractions does not make that focus easy.[7]

The principal must be sure that systems are set up for regular assessment and monitoring of the progress of student achievement. Even with regular assessment, Wiggins (1993, 18) warns, "We fail to regularly adjust performance in light of ongoing results." The principal must guide the process of using the results of assessments to influence staff performance in ways that will make a difference for student progress. In talking about results, the principal must clearly communicate an expectation of promoting student success to the learning community.

Schmoker (1996) states that the discussion of results in itself promotes a sharpening of focus and a sure sense of purpose for a school. Principals must rise above the daily tasks to provide leadership in assessing results and helping focus the school on it central purpose—student achievement.

SHOWING APPRECIATION AND CELEBRATING ACCOMPLISHMENTS

The principal must show appreciation and praise success for both individuals and groups. Any school has individual teachers and groups who are working hard to reach school goals. All need to have others show appreciation. All need signs that others recognize their accomplishments. A principal and others in a school can become so involved in their work they forget to stop and celebrate accomplishments as they strive to reach their goals. Individuals and groups will cherish recognition for their work and their dedication to achieving the school vision. The principal must set up ongoing practices to show appreciation to individuals as well as groups on a periodic basis. These practices will help end the isolation and anonymity of individuals working in the school. Recognition highlights what matters for school success and

---

[7] Reprinted with permission of Association for Supervision and Curriculum Development from *Results: The Key to Continuous School Improvement*, 103, by Mike Schmoker. © 1996 by Association for Supervision and Curriculum Development.

helps reinforce the learning community culture. Wheatley (1994) in *Leadership and the New Science* emphasizes the importance of the principal's leadership role in recognizing efforts:

> Leaders, then, must be broadcasters, targeting praise and recognition to create a unified, purposeful culture. (p. 66)

Further, Schmoker (1996) emphasizes the importance of recognition in building a school learning community:

> Developing a positive, productive, and fulfilling field in a school or district means providing contexts and flashpoints that promote positive and productive thoughts and conversations. If we frequently clarify and celebrate progress towards goals and the impact of our efforts on students, we help sustain the conditions essential to a healthy, ever-improving workplace. Just as important are efforts to recognize, reward, and celebrate accomplishments, which work preemptively to ward off the destructive thoughts and conversations that are the inevitable result when an organization ignores the social and psychological needs of its people.[8]

A principal should provide regular occasions to recognize, celebrate, and reward the meaningful accomplishments of individuals and groups within the learning community, thus sustaining and nourishing the school vision. These occasions keep the school aware of its central purpose and goals. The principal as leader must understand the enormous impact of recognition on all members of the learning community. The principal must be aware that recognition reinforces the central work of the learning community. Recognizing what matters reinforces the vision of the school and what is held important.

TAKING CARE OF STAFF, STUDENTS, AND COMMUNITY

Being supportive and caring about people are important qualities in a leader. The principal must take care of and support teachers, staff, students, and the rest of the community. Individuals work better under conditions where they know people care about them as people and not just about their work. Schools are intense places to work with lots of

---

[8] Ibid, 107.

human interactions, and a sense of caring can sustain individual efforts as well as whole school efforts. As with recognition, if people know that the leader cares about their work and their individual lives, that knowledge reinforces their sense of commitment and purpose for working in the school. A caring environment can help sustain a school through tough times. A sense of community emerges from an environment where individuals have a concern about what happens to one another. Taking care of individuals and the entire learning community is an important aspect of the principal's daily work. Individuals within the school will not function well when there is a lack of caring, support, and concern shown by the principal. No one—teachers, staff, or students—tends to perform well in schools where a caring environment does not exist.

MOTIVATING ALL PEOPLE IN THE SCHOOL COMMUNITY

As a leader, the principal must find ways to motivate people and the school community to help reach the school's goals. Motivation is necessary to sustain continuous improvement within a school. Understanding motivation factors helps a principal develop strategies and plans for bringing about change. Motivating factors vary from individual to individual, and principals must employ a variety of incentives to motivate staff individually and collectively. The principal should conduct periodic reviews of what motivates and inspires the staff members and the school community.

USING HUMAN SKILLS (INTERPERSONAL AND GROUP)

The principalship is a people-oriented position that requires interpersonal and group skills to work with a variety of issues, groups, and individuals to realize the community's vision for the school. The principal must engage others in dialogue and institute processes that promote and create interaction among individuals and groups. Using decision-making skills and developing consensus are key to establishing a school learning community culture. If the school is to improve student performance, then the principal must have a variety of interpersonal and group skills to work with individuals and groups to bring about change and move the school closer to its vision.

SUMMARY

The leader role is a pivotal aspect of the principalship that sets the beliefs of the educator into action. As a leader, the principal must foster development of the school learning community by empowering others to act, based on the vision of the school. Through appraising, envisioning, empowering, communicating, and building trust, a principal as leader helps the members of the learning community create a school that reflects common values and works toward improved student achievement. The leadership of the principal is a key factor in establishing and nurturing this learning community on a daily basis.

REFLECTIVE ACTIVITIES

1. Shadow a Principal for a Day

Shadow a principal for a day to watch for interactions in the leadership role. Given the content of this text, other readings, and your course work, prepare interview questions on leadership to ask the principal at the end of the day. Summarize the important points from your observation and interview on leadership of the principalship. Be prepared to discuss them in class.

2. Expectation for the Principal's Leadership by Teachers

Given what you now know about the leadership role of the principal, interview three teachers at your school regarding their perceptions of the principal's leadership role. Summarize their responses and comment on what insights you gained about the perceptions of the principal's role as leader from a teacher's perspective.

3. Principal's Reflective Practice Model

Using the Principal's Reflective Practice Model described in this chapter, interview a principal about reflecting on practices and the leadership role. Explain the model and ask what sources the principal uses to reflect on current practices.

SUGGESTED READINGS

Bennis, Warren, and Burt Nanus. 1985. *Leaders: The Strategies for Taking Charge*. New York: Harper and Row.

Sergiovanni, Thomas J. 1995. *The Principalship: A Reflective Practice Perspective*. 3d ed. Boston: Allyn and Bacon.

Short, Paula M., and John T. Greer. 1997. *Leadership in Empowered Schools: Themes from Innovative Efforts*. Upper Saddle River, NJ: Merrill/Prentice Hall.

Smith, Stuart C., and Philip K. Piele, eds. 1996. *School Leadership: Handbook for Excellence*. 3d ed. Eugene, OR: ERIC Clearinghouse on Educational Management, University of Oregon.

REFERENCES

Barth, Roland. 1990. *Improving Schools from Within*. San Francisco: Jossey-Bass.

Bennis, Warren, and Burt Nanus. 1985. *Leaders: The Strategies for Taking Charge*. New York: Harper and Row.

Kouzes, James M., and Barry Z. Posner. 1995. *The Leadership Challenge: How to Keep Getting Extraordinary Things Done in Organizations*. San Francisco: Jossey-Bass.

Lashway, Larry. 1996. Leadership Styles and Strategies. In *School Leadership: Handbook for Excellence,* edited by Stuart C. Smith and Philip K. Piele. 3d ed. Eugene, OR: ERIC Clearinghouse on Educational Management, University of Oregon.

Schmoker, Mike. 1996. *Results: The Key to Continuous School Improvement*. Alexandria, VA: Association for Supervision and Curriculum Development.

Senge, Peter, Art Kliener, Charlotte Roberts, Richard B. Ross, and Bryan J. Smith. 1994. *The Fifth Discipline Fieldbook: Strategies and Tools for Building a Learning Organization.* New York: Doubleday.

Sergiovanni, Thomas J. 1995. *The Principalship: A Reflective Practice Perspective.* 3d ed. Boston: Allyn and Bacon.

Short, Paula M., and John T. Greer. 1997. *Leadership in Empowered Schools: Themes from Innovative Efforts.* Upper Saddle River, NJ: Merrill/Prentice Hall.

Wheatley, Margaret. 1994. *Leadership and the New Science.* San Francisco, CA: Berrett-Koehler Publishers.

Wiggins, Grant. 1993. *Assessing Student Performance: Exploring the Purpose and Limits of Testing.* San Francisco, CA: Jossey-Bass.

CHAPTER 4

PRINCIPAL AS MANAGER

As a new principal, you are asked to handle many different managerial tasks throughout the day. You are trying to provide leadership, but continually get bogged down in the many management duties required for the school to operate effectively and efficiently. What management tasks must a new principal be aware of and perform? How do you see your role as manager versus that of leader in building a successful learning community in your school? How will you develop your management role as principal?

THE ROLE OF THE MANAGER

The role of the principal as manager (see Figure 4.1) is key in the daily organizing, functioning, and execution of numerous processes and tasks that permit a school to accomplish its goals as a learning community. As the school's chief manager, the principal develops systems to manage the school effectively and efficiently. The management role includes the routine behaviors and tasks that must take place daily

FIGURE 4.1
The Principal as
Manager

Manager Role

- Preparing and planning
- Organizing
- Managing through recurring systems
- Directing and carrying out
- Evaluating and improving

within a school for it to operate. The principal's manager role includes preparing, planning, providing resources, scheduling and monitoring, budgeting and bookkeeping, maintaining facilities, handling student problems, and keeping a safe environment.

Effective management helps a school achieve its goals, in part by making the school function well enough to allow the leadership role of the principalship to emerge.

Smith and Piele (1996) summarize the importance of the management aspect of the principalship:

> School leaders must first of all be skillful managers. . . . Whatever else a district may want from its leaders, managerial skill is essential; without it, no school leader will last long. (p. 15)

Managerial competence is a clear expectation that districts, teachers, parents, and communities have of the principal. A principal exemplifies good management practices through the systematic application of an array of management skills to provide for an orderly and efficient school environment. Such an environment enables students to learn and staff members to provide optimum learning opportunities. A well-managed school allows students to spend more time on learning.

The National Association of Secondary School Principals (NASSP) research studies and assessment reports describe what principals must do and be good at to effectively manage schools. The 1988 NASSP research results, as cited in Ubben and Hughes (1992), reveal six abilities important to successful school administration:

- The ability to plan and organize work
- The ability to work with and lead others
- The ability to analyze problems and make decisions
- The ability to communicate orally and in writing

■ The ability to perceive the needs and concerns of others

■ The ability to perform under pressure. (p. 9)[1]

Effectively carrying out the managerial role enhances the principal's leadership ability to help change and improve the school. Hughes (1994) defines the principal's management role as encompassing productive efforts to manage a status quo in which people can work comfortably.

Sergiovanni (1991) provides a perspective on the relationship between the management and leadership roles of the principalship:

> Distinctions between management and leadership are useful for theorists and help to clarify and sort various activities and behaviors of principals. For practical purposes, however, both emphases should be considered as necessary and important aspects of a principal's administrative style. The choice is not whether a principal is leader or manager but whether the two emphases are in balance and, indeed, whether they complement each other. (p. 16)

Thus, the principal's managerial role is essential in paving the way for leadership initiatives in building a learning community that optimizes learning for students, teachers, and staff members.

In reviewing the roles of the principal, it is important to note the conclusions of Morris and his colleagues in *Principals in Action: The Reality of Managing Schools* (1984), a study of principals and their work:

> The principalship is a moving, dynamic occupation. . . . The rhythm of the job, from arrival at the parking lot to the close of the business day, is typified by pace and movement, by frequent and abrupt shifts from one concern to another, and by the excitement pervading any institution dealing with young people. . . . The principal's job is different from other managerial positions because it is essentially an oral occupation, a job of talking. The principal governs the school mostly by talking with other people, usually one at a time, throughout the day. (p. 209)

The complex nature of the principal's managerial work is characterized by brevity, variety, and fragmentation. The managerial activities are not only varied, but also without patterns, disconnected, and interspersed with trivia. The principal must often switch to a different mood or frame of mind simply to carry out the tasks. Today's principal is compelled to perform a greater number of tasks at an unrelenting pace.

Barth (1980) describes the range of responsibilities, including those of a manager, that principals face:

---

[1] NASSP has many relevant reports. For information, contact the National Association of Secondary School Principals, 1904 Association Drive, Reston, VA 22091.

The principal is ultimately responsible for almost everything that happens in school and out. We are responsible for personnel—making sure that employees are physically present and working to the best of their ability. We are in charge of programs—making sure that teachers are teaching what they are supposed to and that children are learning it. We are accountable to parents—making sure that each is given an opportunity to express problems and that those problems are addressed and resolved. We are expected to protect the physical safety of children—making sure that the several hundred lively organisms who leave each morning return, equally lively, in the afternoon.

Over the years, principals have assumed one small additional responsibility after another—responsibility for the safe passage of children from school to home, responsibility for making sure the sidewalks are plowed of snow in winter, responsibility for health education, sex education, moral education, responsibility for teaching children to evacuate school buses and to ride their bikes safely. We have taken on lunch programs, then breakfast programs; responsibility for the physical condition of the furnace, the wiring, the playground equipment. We are now accountable for children's achievement of minimum standards at each grade level, for the growth of children with special needs, of the gifted, and of those who are neither. The principal has become a provider of social services, food services, health care, recreation programs and transportation—with a solid skills education worked in somehow. (pp. 4–6)

The tremendous number of tasks makes the managerial role of the principal highly open-ended. A key to the principalship is to use this aspect of the job to set priorities for management as well as leadership and then to pursue those priorities to improve the school learning community.

PREPARING AND PLANNING

In developing a school environment where students can learn and teachers can teach, the principal as manager must monitor and direct the school's daily operations and overall environment. Carrying out the role of manager means that the principal must plan for the many events that will recur, such as scheduling classes and dealing with disciplinary matters, and must also prepare for unexpected matters that will inevitably arise. Careful preparation and planning will help make the school run smoothly. Without proper preparation and planning, the school cannot accomplish even basic tasks, such as scheduling students or implementing a new curriculum. Unless the principal provides clear direction and support, planning and preparation ordinarily will not take place at all. For a school to operate well and meet the needs of students, teachers, staff, and parents, a learning community must have the fundamental preparation and planning.

Lunenburg (1995) in *The Principalship: Concepts and Applications* discusses the importance of planning as a part of the managerial role of the principalship:

> Planning is important because it provides organization members a sense of purpose and direction, outlines the kinds of tasks they will be performing and explains how their activities are related to the overall goals of the school. . . . Without this information, employees would not know precisely how to use their time and energies efficiently and effectively. Subsequently, they would respond to their job responsibilities randomly, wasting valuable human resources. (p. 6)

Principals are often criticized by teachers, staff, parents, and others in the community for failing to plan and prepare. This ability is a key managerial skill for any principal.

ORGANIZING

Principals who are good managers must have strong organizational skills. The multitude of activities and deadlines that occur throughout the school year require the principal to organize, monitor, and carry out multiple tasks every day. Without the necessary organizational skills, the principal would have a school in chaos. Within a learning community, the principal should help organize and involve others in carrying out tasks that help accomplish the mission and goals of the school. A principal who organizes well has more time to set priorities, devote time to important matters, and work with others in the learning community.

Lunenburg (1995) sees organizing as involving three essential elements for the principalship: developing the structure of the organization, acquiring and training staff members, and establishing patterns and networks. As Lunenburg describes it:

> In a very basic sense, designing the structure of the organization involves creating the organizational chart for a school. The principal establishes policies and procedures for authority relationships, reporting patterns, the chain of command, departmentalization, and various administrative and subordinate responsibilities. Then the principal takes steps to hire competent personnel. When necessary, the principal establishes programs for training new personnel in the skills necessary to carry out their task assignments. Finally, the principal builds

formal communication and information networks, including the types of information to be communicated, direction of communication flows, and reduction in barriers to effective communications. (p. 7)

The ability of the principal to organize a learning community with the necessary systems and structures to work together is critical to the ongoing functioning of the organization. A school learning community must be organized in such a way that it promotes interaction, reflection, and development. The principal's managerial role in achieving this is a critical component.

MANAGING THROUGH RECURRING SYSTEMS

The principal is responsible for setting up management of recurring systems that make the school run effectively and efficiently for teachers, students, and staff. Examples of a school's recurring systems include bell schedules, regular meetings, awards ceremonies, discipline procedures, textbook and supply inventories, budgets, and cafeteria, custodial, and transportation services. Individuals in the learning community need to count on these recurring systems, and having them establishes a sense of stability and predictability that allows the learning community to function effectively. Dependable, recurring systems allow people to develop trust that things will happen according to established policies and procedures. The stability of the school's ongoing managerial functions provide a foundation for the development of the learning community's work. Trust in the principal's managerial skills is crucial to the learning community environment.

DIRECTING AND CARRYING OUT

The involvement of a variety of stakeholders in building a learning community is important, but a principal's failure to direct and institute the decisions and efforts of its members will result in inconsistency and a credibility gap. In the manager role, the principal needs to ensure direction and the ability to carry out the agreed-on policies and procedures that the learning community has developed.

In a study of principals, Morris et al. (1984) note that principals spend about half their time outside the main office and describe the principal's manager role this way:

A busy principal covers a great deal of ground. In making these rounds, from office to corridor to classroom to gymnasium to boiler room to playground and back, the principal is managing the school. But it is management in a form unusual for most organizations because it is, in large part, administration at the work stations of other persons. This means that the principal carries the office around with him or her through at least 50% of the work day. . . . It is the principal who gets around, who visits teachers in their offices, who investigates areas of potential trouble, who smoothes the flow of messages from one area of the building to another, who is on call and easily summoned by those needing assistance. (p. 211)

EVALUATING AND IMPROVING

Even while working with a variety of management systems, policies, and procedures, the principal must continually evaluate the school with an eye toward improving it. This means setting up processes to question whether a system is working as intended. The feedback can help the principal avoid the pitfall of accepting things as they are—a failing that is unacceptable in building a learning community. A principal needs to stop periodically to evaluate actions.

REFLECTIONS: THIS ONGOING EVALUATION CAN FOSTER THE DIS-
CUSSIONS AMONG MEMBERS OF THE LEARNING COMMUNITY
THAT KEEP EVERYONE FOCUSED ON THEIR VISION OF THE SCHOOL
AND WHETHER PROGRESS IS BEING MADE TOWARD THAT VISION.
AS A PRINCIPAL, HOW WOULD YOU FOSTER THIS ONGOING EVALU-
ATION PROCESS? TAKE TIME TO WRITE DOWN YOUR THOUGHTS.

SUMMARY

The manager role of the principalship requires the principal to be able to prepare, plan, organize, and manage recurring systems, to direct and carry out decisions, and evaluate and improve the school's overall operation. Good management is the foundation on which a school learning community can be built. The principal's management skills—good or bad—determine whether the school will run effectively and efficiently.

REFLECTIVE ACTIVITIES

1. Management Role of the Principal

Interview a principal about the management role of the principalship. What insights did you gain about the principal's perspectives on managing a school? Prepare a written summary.

2. Choose a Management Role to Investigate in Depth

Choose one of the management roles described in this chapter—for example, preparing, planning, organizing, managing through recurring systems, or directing and carrying out—to study in depth with a principal. First shadow and then interview a principal with prepared questions regarding the specific management role. Report on the insights you gained about this management role as applied by the principal you observed.

SUGGESTED READINGS

Hughes, Larry. 1994. *The Principal as Leader.* Upper Saddle River, NJ: Merrill/Prentice Hall.

Keith, Sherry, and Robert Henriques Girling. 1991. *Education, Management, and Participation: New Directions in Educational Administration.* Boston: Allyn and Bacon.

Lunenburg, Fred C. 1995. *The Principalship: Concepts and Applications.* Upper Saddle River, NJ: Merrill/Prentice Hall.

Smith, Stuart C., and Philip K. Piele, eds. 1996. *School Leadership: Handbook for Excellence.* 2d ed. Eugene, OR: ERIC Clearinghouse on Educational Management, University of Oregon.

REFERENCES

Barth, Roland. 1980. Reflections on the Principalship. *Thrust for Educational Leadership* 9(5): 4–6.

Hughes, Larry. 1994. *The Principal as Leader.* Upper Saddle River, NJ: Merrill/Prentice Hall.

Lunenburg, Fred C. 1995. *The Principalship: Concepts and Applications.* Upper Saddle River, NJ: Merrill/Prentice Hall.

Morris, Van Cleve, Robert L. Crowson, Cynthia Porter-Gehrie, and Emmanuel Hurwitz, Jr. 1984. *Principals in Action: The Reality of Managing Schools.* Columbus, OH: Merrill.

Sergiovanni, Thomas J. 1991. *The Principalship: A Reflective Practice Perspective.* 2d ed. Boston: Allyn and Bacon.

Smith, Stuart C., and Philip K. Piele, eds. 1996. *School Leadership: Handbook for Excellence.* 2d ed. Eugene, OR: ERIC Clearinghouse on Educational Management, University of Oregon.

Ubben, Gerald C., and Larry W. Hughes. 1992. *The Principal: Creative Leadership for Effective Schools.* 2d ed. Boston: Allyn and Bacon.

CHAPTER 5

PRINCIPAL'S INNER PERSON

Inner Person Role

Clarifying Personal Beliefs About Schooling and Learning

Making Commitments to Schooling and Learning

Acting Ethically and Honestly

Developing and Practicing Good Habits of Physical and Emotional Health

Balancing Life

Planning for Financial Security

Enjoying Family, Friends, and Social and Cultural Activities

Reading Widely and Keeping Professionally Updated

Reflecting on Practice

Tolerating an Ambiguous World

Tapping Inner Resources for Strength and Humor

PROBLEM SCENARIO

As a first-year principal, you are extremely busy and constantly learning about a variety of issues facing your school. The role of principal has begun to create stress in your life and drain your energy like no other job you have had before. Ethical dilemmas, time commitments, expectations, and other demands of the school, as well as family obligations, have begun to strain your capacity to deal with the sheer volume of a principal's duties. What resources and sources of strength do you have to continue your commitment to the principalship and building a school learning community? How can you take care of yourself so that you can do the best job possible for your school and keep a healthy, balanced personal and professional life?

INNER PERSON ROLE

The inner person role (see Figure 5.1) represents the center of the Principalship Model (see Figure 5.2), where the educator, manager, and leader roles mesh to define a principal's character and values. The inner person element embraces the beliefs, commitment, and internal

Inner Person Role

- Clarifying personal beliefs about schooling and learning
- Making commitments to schooling and learning
- Acting ethically and honestly
- Developing and practicing good habits of physical and emotional health
- Balancing life
- Planning for financial security
- Enjoying family, friends, and social and cultural activities
- Reading widely and keeping professionally updated
- Reflecting on practice
- Tolerating an ambiguous world
- Tapping inner resources for strength and humor

FIGURE 5.1
The Principal as Inner Person

balance that a principal must maintain to be able to focus on building a school learning community when faced with the mounting stresses and strains of daily work.

The inner person role requires the principal to clarify beliefs on educational philosophy, commitment to education, and social and moral issues affecting the school community. The inner person raises issues of ethics, honesty, and humane actions as well as the need for good habits of physical and emotional health. The inner person aspect of the Principalship Model calls for the principal to keep a balanced and healthy personal and professional lifestyle that includes enjoying family and friends, planning for financial security, reading widely and keeping professionally updated, participating culturally in the community, tapping inner strengths, and not only tolerating an ambiguous world but also keeping a sense of humor and amazement regarding it. Exploring the inner person as an aspect of the principalship provides perspective on how a principal develops, gains confidence, and commits to daily school duties while keeping a balanced life.

FIGURE 5.2
Principalship Model

CLARIFYING PERSONAL BELIEFS ABOUT SCHOOLING AND LEARNING

The inner person role requires the principal to clarify beliefs about how students learn and how to work with others in the school learning community to improve the quality of life and learning for students. The inner person holds the core beliefs that the principal has developed over time and through experiences as an educator. The principal must hold a strong educational philosophy to lean on when facing the issues confronting the school. This will provide a sense of focus, giving meaning, consistency, and purpose to the principal's actions. People working with the principal want to know where the principal stands on issues of learning. They want to know that the principal's core beliefs will hold firm against pressure and provide consistency.

If you were a principal, how would you clarify your beliefs about schooling so that the school learning community receives a clear and consistent message about what you believe? To help you think about your educational philosophy, here are some questions that you should ponder:

What does a student need to know and be able to do?

What would best prepare students for the future?

How should students be able to think?

What should students value and believe?

How should students inquire, learn, and work together?

How should teachers, administrators, and students interact?

What conditions are best for students to learn and teachers to teach?

What is the role of the teacher?

What do you believe about how students learn?

How do the adults in the school work together?

How does the community work with the school?

What is the role of a parent in schooling?

What do you believe about educational accountability?

What is the role of the principal in a school?

How do you define a school learning community?

As a principal, you must not only clarify beliefs about schooling and learning, but also put these beliefs into practice daily. The school learning community will soon realize through your actions what you hold important about schooling and learning. As a principal, you must remember that your core beliefs must guide your actions. Commitment to these beliefs will sustain your efforts to improve the school.

Without fervent commitment to a personal educational philosophy, the principal will drift aimlessly. The school will follow suit if the principal does not have and adhere to a coherent set of beliefs. The principal whose work is meaningful with a deep sense of purpose and commitment is less likely to be overwhelmed by the principalship.

Greenfield (1985) concluded from extensive studies of the principalship and school leadership that principals need to be passionate about their work, clear about what they seek to accomplish, and aggressive in searching for understanding that leads to improved schooling.

Greenfield (1985) describes passion for the principalship as:

> believing in the worth of what one seeks to accomplish and exhibiting in one's daily action a commitment to the realization of those goals and purposes. (p. 17)

A principal's sense of clarity about purpose and goals is key. Blumberg and Greenfield (1980) concluded from their research that principals who lead tend to be highly goal-oriented and have a keen sense of clarity about their goals.

Barth (1990) further emphasizes the need for principals to have a real sense of values and strong commitment to a personal vision:

> Without a vision, I think our behavior becomes reflexive, inconsistent, and shortsighted as we seek the action that will put out the fire fastest so we can get on with putting out the next one. In five years, if we are lucky, our school might be fire free—but it will not have changed much. Anxiety will remain high, humor low, and leadership muddled. Or, as one teacher put it in a powerful piece of writing, "Without a clear sense of purpose we get lost, and our activities in school become but empty vessels of our discontent." Seafaring folk put it differently: "For the sailor without a destination, there is no favorable wind."[1]

Barth (1990) concedes that a problem for many principals is that their vision is usually "deeply submerged, sometimes fragmentary, and seldom articulated" (p. 148). Barth suggests that the vision begins to

---

[1] Reprinted with permission of Jossey-Bass Inc. from *Improving Schools from Within,* 177, by Roland Barth. © 1990 by Jossey-Bass Inc., Publishers.

re-emerge when leaders force themselves to complete open-ended statements like:

- When I leave this school I would like to be remembered for . . .
- I want my place to be a school where . . .
- The kind of school I would like my children to attend would . . .
- The kind of school I would like to teach in . . . [2]

These are not insignificant statements for a principal, nor are they easy to answer. Personal vision and values are important when the principal runs up against bureaucratic procedures and mandates that test one's beliefs. Being grounded in personal beliefs provides a principal with a sound foundation for working with a variety of individuals to build a learning community that meets students' needs. This is the heart of the principalship because it is what a principal believes, values, dreams about, and is committed to—a personal vision.

REFLECTIONS: TAKE SOME TIME NOW TO CLARIFY YOUR BELIEFS ABOUT SCHOOLING. HOW WOULD YOU AS PRINCIPAL ANSWER THE PREVIOUS OPEN-ENDED QUESTIONS? WHAT WOULD YOU SAY TO YOUR TEACHERS, STUDENTS, PARENTS, AND THE REST OF THE COMMUNITY REGARDING YOUR EDUCATIONAL PHILOSO- PHY AND PERSONAL VISION FOR SCHOOLING? HOW WOULD THEY SEE IT IN YOUR ACTIONS? WRITE DOWN YOUR THOUGHTS, INCLUDING A PERSONAL VISION STATEMENT.

As the role of the principalship unfolds, there sometimes are blocks to clarifying a personal vision. Bennis, Parikh, and Lessem (1994) suggest a number of causes of such blocks to a clear vision:

- Being too focused on daily routines. (The concreteness of the daily routine tempts one away from the more ambiguous challenge of developing vision.)
- Wanting to be just one of the crowd. (A bold vision is risky; it calls attention to oneself and creates new expectations.)

---

[2] Ibid, 148. [Bullets added for clarity.]

■ Flitting from one thing to the other. (Some people are overwhelmed by possibilities; in trying to cover everything, they end
  up without a clear focus on anything.)

■ Reckless risk-taking. (Some leaders enjoy a high-wire act in
  which they are the stars.)

■ Clinging to established principles to avoid ambiguity. (Creating
  a new future is filled with uncertainty; some leaders just tinker
  around the margins.)

■ Being too open-minded. (Some leaders find it difficult to choose.)

■ Believing you have all the answers. (In their hearts, some leaders simply don't believe that major change is needed.) (p. 142)

In reviewing these blocks to developing a vision, a principal can
identify factors that help or hinder the development and movement
toward achieving a personal vision. A principal's vision and beliefs
have a powerful effect on a school learning community because they
help create meaning in the life of the school, attract the commitment
of followers, and provide meaning for the work of the school.

Leithwood, Begley, and Cousins (1994) summarize the importance of a leader's vision from their research:

> A blurred vision offers little guidance for school-leaders and their
> colleagues. (p. 41)

MAKING COMMITMENTS TO
SCHOOLING AND LEARNING

The principal must show commitment to schooling through personal
beliefs and actions. School communities and teachers have seen principals come and go in their schools. What kind of commitment should a
principal make to a school learning community? What kind of commitment should a principal expect from the community in return? The
issue of commitment for a principal is a critical one. This two-way commitment is especially needed during stressful times at the school when
it can sustain people faced with difficult issues. Principals must know
where they stand in relation to their commitment to certain actions and
beliefs. As the school year unfolds, various issues will test the principal's commitment. The school's administrative team and others in the
learning community must understand the depth of the principal's commitment and willingness to work toward fulfillment of the vision. It is
not the principal's commitment alone that is important, but how that

commitment is built with others within the school learning community. The principal must be the builder as well as keeper of the commitment to improving the quality of life and learning for every student.

Sergiovanni (1995) summarizes the importance of a principal's outward display of commitment in supporting the daily efforts of all in the school:

> One of the great secrets of leadership is that before one can command the respect and followership of others, she or he must demonstrate devotion to the organization's purposes and commitment to those in the organization who work day to day on the ordinary tasks that are necessary for the those purposes to be realized. (p. 320)

Further, Peters and Austin (1985) in *A Passion for Excellence*, a study of the corporate world, express the importance of commitment and passion:

> We see that excellence is achieved by people who muster up the nerve (and the passion) to step out—in spite of doubt, or fear, or job description. They won't retreat behind office doors, committees, memos or layers of staff, knowing this is the fair bargain they make for extraordinary results. . . . Courage and self-respect are the lion's share of passion: it's hanging in long after others have gotten bored or given up; it's refusing to leave well enough alone; it means that anything less than the best you can imagine really bothers you, maybe keeps you awake at night. It usually means sticking your neck out: daring to give your best shot to something you care about and asking others to do the same is self-exposing. It asks you to pick sides, to wear your passion on your sleeve, to take a position and remain true to it even under the scrutiny of an audience, when the wish to please, to be accepted, welcomed, can compromise the clearest inner vision. (pp. 414–15)

REFLECTIONS: HOW DO YOU SEE COMMITMENT AND PASSION

FOR SCHOOLING AND LEARNING? CAN YOU DESCRIBE YOUR VIEW

USING THE PERSONAL VISION STATEMENT THAT YOU FORMU-

LATED EARLIER IN THIS CHAPTER? HOW WOULD YOUR SCHOOL

LEARNING COMMUNITY SEE THAT COMMITMENT UNFOLD IN YOUR

DAILY PRACTICE AS A PRINCIPAL? WRITE DOWN YOUR THOUGHTS.

ACTING ETHICALLY AND HONESTLY

The principal must deal ethically with others in the school learning community. Principals face ethical dilemmas regarding schooling daily through demands and requests from teachers, students, parents, and the rest of the community. Principals can lose respect with actions that are not ethical, fair, and honest. In dealing with matters of ethics, the principal continues to clarify personal beliefs and demonstrate a commitment to those beliefs.

What types of ethics and honesty issues might confront a principal? The following example illustrates an ethics issue that a principal might face.

> *A parent asks a principal to transfer a child from a certain classroom because the teacher verbally abuses the children. The principal talks with the parent, child, and teacher to investigate the allegations. The principal knows that other classrooms are full and that the teacher in question has drawn complaints previously, but none recently. The principal decides that the child will not be moved, infuriating the parent. A school board member with a child in the same class approaches the principal with a similar request for a transfer. How should the principal handle the board member's request, considering the board member's status in the learning community? The superintendent has called to see how the principal will handle the situation because the board member has informed the superintendent of misgivings about the teacher. All the teachers are curious about what decision the principal will make regarding the board member's request.*

REFLECTIONS: HOW WOULD YOU HANDLE THIS ETHICS SITUATION

AS A PRINCIPAL? WHAT QUESTIONS WOULD YOU ASK? WHAT ADDI-

TIONAL INFORMATION WOULD YOU WANT? WHAT BELIEFS WOULD

AFFECT YOUR DECISION? HOW FIRMLY WOULD YOU STAND ON

YOUR BELIEFS WHEN QUESTIONED BY THE SUPERINTENDENT OR

THE BOARD MEMBER? WRITE DOWN YOUR THOUGHTS.

Successful leadership and administrative practices depend largely on the principal's ethics. Honesty and ethical behaviors guide the principal's actions and demonstrate the sense of purpose and commitment that a school learning community expects from a principal. Thus, principals must be clear about their core beliefs to be consistent and fair in their daily actions in a school.

DEVELOPING AND PRACTICING GOOD HABITS OF PHYSICAL AND EMOTIONAL HEALTH

Reasoner (1995) highlights the impact of job stress on administrators today:

> Today's school administrators need a new set of survival skills to avoid mental and physical problems associated with the job. Feelings of burnout, depression, and loss of control are becoming increasingly common among administrators. (p. 28)

Developing and practicing good habits of physical and emotional health provide the principal as administrator with a necessary balance in the hectic pace of the principalship. Regular exercise, no matter what type, keeps the principal physically fit, helping to overcome the energy-sapping stress of the job. Physical activity can boost a principal's productivity by relieving stress through exercise.

REFLECTIONS: AS A NEW OR FUTURE PRINCIPAL, WHAT VALUE DO YOU SEE IN KEEPING A REGULAR EXERCISE PROGRAM TO HELP YOU DO YOUR JOB BETTER AND KEEP A BALANCE IN YOUR LIFE? HOW WOULD YOU FIND THE TIME TO PURSUE THAT EXERCISE PROGRAM? THINK ABOUT THIS AND LOOK AT CURRENT PRACTICES OF PRINCIPALS. WRITE DOWN YOUR THOUGHTS.

BALANCING LIFE

Besides keeping physically fit, the principal must keep a balance between work and life outside the school. Most principals find the job imposes demands that interfere with normal family life and personal time. The job never seems to be done, no matter how many hours they put in. Rather than being driven to seek perfection or approval from others, it is important for principals to determine what they can realistically achieve. Effective principals acknowledge existing conditions and set goals and priorities to focus their energy on matters in which they can make a difference.

Principals should monitor their level of stress and take time to renew their energy when stress rises. Determining what is causing stress is as important as taking action to relieve the stress. Energizing strategies might include closing the office door for a few minutes to meditate, relax, or read; taking a walk around the school or into a classroom; or taking a weekend off from school work. These steps allow the principal to recharge during the daily and weekly bombardment of school issues. In general, a principal must strive to focus on things that warrant attention and dismiss those that do not. Drucker (1966) insists that "the executive's job is to be effective," not efficient, which means getting "the right things done," rather than merely doing things right. Keeping a focus, setting priorities, and managing time effectively help a principal relieve stress and keep emotionally healthy to get the job done well.

PLANNING FOR FINANCIAL SECURITY

Generally, principals pay closer attention to their school budgets than to their own budget plan for financial security. As a principal, it is important to take care of oneself not only physically and mentally, but also financially. Financial planning can add to a sense of security and help relieve stress about personal finances. Oftentimes at the end of a day of taking care of others, a principal may feel too weary to begin planning for financial security yet cannot afford to procrastinate. Just as others must do, a principal must plan for retirement, children's education, recreational activities, and daily and long-term expenses.

Planning for financial security allows principals time to envision their own future. Planning for vacations and other recreational activities can provide an important break from the hectic workday. These breaks can be rejuvenating, providing new levels of energy to deal with the multiple tasks of the principalship.

Principals need to tailor their financial plans to their interests and needs. Good financial planning will give the principal the opportunity to participate in a variety of social, cultural, and recreational activities as well as develop a secure future.

ENJOYING FAMILY, FRIENDS, AND SOCIAL AND CULTURAL ACTIVITIES

Enjoying the company of family, friends, and colleagues on a regular basis permits a principal to relax and enjoy life outside work. Many new principals become obsessed or overwhelmed with their work of the principalship, believing that they must do it all. Engaging in regular social and cultural activities broadens the principal's perspective on the larger world. This not only helps keep the principal from becoming compulsive about work, but also results in a balance for emotional health. Principals must learn to arrange their work and personal calendars so that the work of the principalship does not consume them. These activities represent another way to achieve a healthy balance between work and personal life that is so important for a principal to maintain.

REFLECTIONS: AS A NEW OR FUTURE PRINCIPAL, HOW WOULD YOU KEEP A BALANCE IN YOUR LIFE, PLAN FINANCIALLY, AND ENJOY FAMILY, FRIENDS, AND SOCIAL AND CULTURAL ACTIVITIES? THINK ABOUT THIS AND LOOK AT CURRENT PRACTICES OF PRINCIPALS. WRITE DOWN YOUR THOUGHTS.

READING WIDELY AND KEEPING PROFESSIONALLY UPDATED

Principal should keep informed by reading and associating with others in the profession, in part to be able to act as a professional resource for the school learning community. Professional development for a principal should be a lifelong pursuit because the world of education is constantly changing. Effective principals reflect on their own growth and improvement.

Through professional affiliations and networking with other principals, educators, and community members, a principal can learn new information and perspectives, discover new ways of doing things, and make new connections for resources and sharing ideas. Professional affiliations can help ward off feelings of isolation in a principal. Joining one of the following administrative organizations—addresses are listed after the references at the end of this chapter—is one way a principal can keep updated:

- American Association of School Administrators
- Association for Supervision and Curriculum Development
- National Association of Elementary School Principals
- National Association of Secondary School Principals
- State administrative associations

Further, Reasoner (1995) found that effective principals create their own support groups in which they can share ideas, dreams, and frustrations. Support groups and networks add to a principal's feeling of connectedness, reducing feelings of isolation (Barth 1990). Getting together regularly with fellow principals allows for sharing of ideas, concerns, and pressures of the principalship.

Mentoring and peer coaching for new principals will aid the professional development of the new principals as well as connecting the veteran principal to new practices. Mentoring by experienced principals and administrators lessens a principal's isolation and supports professional learning in ways that focus on the principal's daily work and needs (Caldwell and Carter 1993). Peer coaching, which involves pairing a new principal with one who is new or experienced, is another way for principals to gain support and perspective. As mentioned, the relationships established by mentoring and peer coaching assist in the professional development of both the new principal and the veteran. Sharing ideas with a mentor or peer coach can help a principal gain a broader perspective while getting advice and taking time to reflect on practice. These techniques support opportunities for learning on an individual basis for a principal and fulfill the learning community's expectations of a lifelong learner.

Speck and Krovetz (1996) comment on the importance of peer coaching for a school administrator:

> Peer coaching with a fellow new school administrator provides an excellent opportunity to discuss and reflect on practice in a mutually supportive, safe environment. Debriefing on difficult situations, watching a peer lead meetings, and shadowing a peer during classroom observation are examples of peer coaching activities that allow participants in peer coaching to gain understanding, insight, and support for their administrative work. Unless new school administrators have a structured peer coaching experience, they may rarely find the time to reflect on their practice. (p.38)

To summarize, the benefits of mentoring and peer coaching for a novice principal include:

- reducing isolation among administrators
- building collaborative norms that enable administrators to give and receive ideas and assistance
- spreading successful practices
- transferring university training experiences to the workplace
- understanding the connection between an individual's own planning and organization and the consequences of those actions
- supporting the new administrator through trying circumstances
- encouraging reflective practice

REFLECTING ON PRACTICE

Many principals lack the time to reflect on their actions and put things into perspective. The result is often disillusionment, followed by discouragement, depression, and loss of enthusiasm (Reasoner 1995, 29). The principal must set aside time for inquiry and reflection and engage in these practices with others in the school learning community. Taking the time to reflect on actions and learn from experience will help the principal gain insight and perspective about work. Stopping to think about one's own actions and the course of actions within the school will help the principal understand the progress the school is making toward its vision. Unless a principal spends time reflecting and engaging others in reflection, the school will not be guided by its core principles.

The Principal's Reflective Practice Model introduced in Chapter 3 (Figure 3.3) is important to examine again as it relates to the inner person of the principal. Refer to Figure 5.3 and briefly review the elements of the model that provide sources for reflection on practice leading to confirming or changing practices.

In order to use Sources for Reflective Practice in Figure 5.3, start by choosing an administrative practice that you would like to reflect on. In this example, suppose you decide to reflect on teacher evaluation.

Begin at the bottom of Figure 5.3 with the first level of sources, from Related Knowledge to Exemplary Practice, and describe each area reflecting on the chosen topic, teacher evaluation. In other words, describe what you know about the topic from related knowledge,

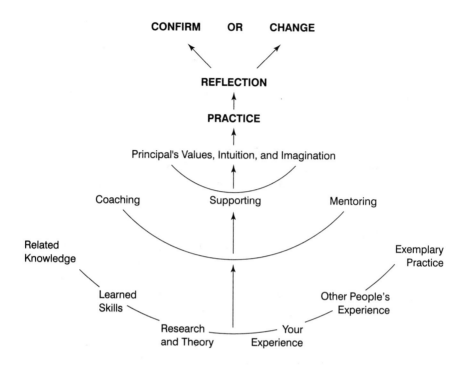

Sources for Reflective Practice

FIGURE 5.3
Principal's Reflective Practice Model

learned skills, research and theory, your experiences, other people's experiences, and exemplary practices. What does each of your descriptions say about your current practice as an administrator?

Now, move up to the next level of sources: Coaching, Supporting, and Mentoring. In what ways have you received or could you receive coaching, support, and mentoring to reflect on your teacher evaluation practices?

Continue to the next step, which is evaluating your own Values, Intuition, and Imagination as a principal as they relate to teacher evaluation. What do these tell you? Now look at your current practice of teacher evaluation. Reflect on it given all the resources you have considered. Decide what should be confirmed and what should be changed. You have now had the opportunity to use this model to reflect on a specific administrative practice.

REFLECTIONS: AS A NEW PRINCIPAL, YOU ARE GIVEN THE TASK

BY THE DISTRICT TO ANALYZE YOUR SCHOOL'S READING PRO-

GRAM. HOW COULD YOU USE THE PRINCIPAL'S REFLECTIVE

PRACTICE MODEL TO HELP YOU ANALYZE YOUR INSTRUCTIONAL

LEADERSHIP ABILITIES AS YOU BEGIN TO LOOK AT THE SCHOOL'S

READING PROGRAM? WRITE DOWN YOUR THOUGHTS USING

EACH LEVEL OF THE MODEL.

As a reflective practitioner, a principal demonstrates the continuous processing of information and issues in various situations. Sergiovanni (1995) provides a perspective regarding reflective practice for the principalship:

> What kind of science is needed that will enable principals to practice successfully in a messy world? The answer is one that resembles a craftlike science, within which professional practice is characterized by interacting reflection and action and episodes. . . . Theory and research are only one source of knowledge, and this knowledge is always subordinate to the principal, teacher, or other professional, serving to inform but not to prescribe practice. Indeed, professional knowledge is created in use as principals and teachers think, reflect, decide, and do. (p. 32)

Schon (1984) describes **reflective practice** as:

> on-the-spot surfacing, criticizing, restructuring and testing of intuitive understandings of experienced phenomenon; often, it takes the form of a reflective conversation with the situation. (p. 65)

Principals need to be able to reflect on the understanding gained from their own or others' actions and add it to their reference for future actions. Included in reflective practice is the use of theory and research as sources of information a principal uses to help increase understanding and informed practice. Reflective principals become students of their practice, informing their professional practice. Thus, principals are continuing to learn and demonstrate as role models the importance of continuous reflection and learning within a learning community.

TOLERATING AN AMBIGUOUS WORLD

Principals must learn to face an ambiguous world and be able to tolerate it and discuss it with others. Working with colleagues in the school, the district, and professional organizations enables a principal to establish a network of individuals and gain perspectives on dealing with the ambiguous world of the principalship and schooling. By talking with others, a principal may gain more positive feelings and reduce stress about work. An isolated principal can lose perspective about what is important and what is trivial. The ambiguities that arise daily within a school can try any principal's patience. Colleagues within the learning community can help clarify issues and situations, thus ending the principal's isolation.

TAPPING INNER RESOURCES FOR STRENGTH AND HUMOR

Keeping a sense of humor and amazement at the way the school and world unfold will keep the principal in a positive state of mind, better able to deal with the unexpected and unwanted occurrences of daily life in the school. Appropriately employed humor can lighten the burdens of the principalship. The ability to laugh and share a humorous event can renew the spirit of a principal, even one who is feeling overwhelmed by the duties of the principalship. Principals need to be able to tap inner resources of strength that will help sustain their work. A sense of commitment and inner source of strength can help a principal encourage the learning community to reach for its vision.

SUMMARY

The strength of the inner person is often overlooked in the development of a person as a principal. It is important that people who assume the role of principal develop and nurture an inner person that will sustain their efforts in building a learning community within their school. The concept of the inner person establishes the importance of commitment, balance, and reflection as an individual carries out the multiple roles of the principalship. By clarifying personal beliefs about schooling and learning, resolving ethics issues, keeping physically and emotionally fit, reflecting on practice and continuing to grow professionally, the person who is becoming a principal will be able to carry out day-to-day duties and enjoy life. Nurturing the inner person is not easy, but it is imperative if the principal is to be truly successful and effective in helping the school learning community grow.

REFLECTIVE ACTIVITIES

1. Discussion with a Principal

Discuss with a principal the main elements of the inner person concept of the Principalship Model as described in this chapter. What insights did you gain about the inner person after your discussion with a principal? What thoughts do you have regarding the inner person for yourself as a future principal? What questions remain for you about the inner person? Be prepared to discuss these insights.

2. Reflective Practice and the Principalship

Through your experiences in education and other areas, what knowledge do you have of reflective practice? How do you see reflective practice used by principals you know or have observed? How important is reflective practice for a principal in building a learning community? If you were a principal, how would you go about the act of reflective practice and making it a daily habit?

SUGGESTED READINGS

Barth, Roland. 1990. *Improving Schools from Within.* San Francisco: Jossey-Bass.

Bennis, Warren, Jagdish Parikh, and Ronnie Lessem. 1994. *Beyond Leadership: Balancing Economics, Ethics, and Ecology.* Cambridge, MA: Blackwell.

Chaleff, Ira. 1995. *The Courageous Follower: Standing Up To and For Our Leaders.* San Francisco: Berrett-Koehler.

Leithwood, Kenneth, Paul T. Begley, and J. Bradley Cousins. 1994. *Developing Expert Leadership for Future Schools*. Washington, DC: Falmer Press.

Schon, Donald A. 1983. *The Reflective Practitioner: How Professionals Think in Action*. New York: Basic Books.

REFERENCES

Barth, Roland. 1990. *Improving Schools from Within*. San Francisco: Jossey-Bass.

Bennis, Warren, Jagdish Parikh, and Ronnie Lessem. 1994. *Beyond Leadership: Balancing Economics, Ethics, and Ecology*. Cambridge, MA: Blackwell.

Blumberg, Arthur, and William Greenfield. 1980. *The Effective Principal: Perspectives on School Leadership*. Boston: Allyn and Bacon.

Caldwell, Brian J., and Earl M. A. Carter. 1993. *The Return of the Mentor: Strategies for Workplace Learning*. London: Falmer Press.

Drucker, Peter. 1966. *The Effective Executive*. New York: Harper and Row.

Greenfield, William. 1985. "Instructional Leadership: Muddles, Puzzles, and Promises." Athens, GA: The Doyne M. Smith Lecture, University of Georgia, June 29.

Leithwood, Kenneth, Paul T. Begley, and J. Bradley Cousins. 1994. *Developing Expert Leadership for Future Schools*. Washington, DC: Falmer Press.

Peters, Tom, and Nancy Austin. 1985. *A Passion for Excellence*. New York: Random House.

Reasoner, Robert W. 1995. Survival Skills for Administrators. *Thrust for Educational Leadership* 24(6): 28–31.

Schon, Donald A. 1984. Leadership as Reflection in Action. In *Leadership and Organizational Culture*, edited by Thomas J. Sergiovanni and John E. Corbally, 64–72. Urbana-Champaign, IL: University of Illinois Press.

Sergiovanni, Thomas J. 1995. *The Principalship: A Reflective Practice Perspective*. 3d ed. Boston: Allyn and Bacon.

Speck, Marsha, and Martin Krovetz. 1996. Developing Effective Peer Coaching Experiences for School Administrators. *ERS Spectrum-Journal of School Research and Information* 14(1): 37–42.

PROFESSIONAL ADMINISTRATIVE ASSOCIATIONS

National Associations

American Association of School Administrators
1801 North Main St.
Arlington, VA 22209
703-528-0700
Fax: 703-841-1543
E-mail: membership@aasa.org
Web page: www.aasa.org

Association for Supervision and Curriculum Development
1250 N. Pitt St.
Alexandria, VA 22314–1433
800–933–2723
703–549–9110
Fax: 703–299–8631
E-mail: member@ascd.org
Web page: www.ascd.org

National Association of Elementary School Principals
1615 Duke Street
Alexandria, VA 22314–3483
800–386–2377
Fax: 800-39-naesp
E-mail: naesp@naesp.org
Web page: www.naesp.org

National Association of Secondary School Principals
1904 Association Drive
Reston, VA 20191–1537
703–860–0200
Fax: 703–476–5432
E-mail: tierney@nassp.org
Web page: www.nassp.org

State Administrative Associations

The following is one example of the many state associations:

Association of California School Administrators
1575 Bayshore Highway
Burlingame, CA 94010
415–692–4300
800–672–3494
E-mail: member@acsa.org
Web page: www.acsa.org

International Associations

The following is one example of an international association:

The International Network of Principals' Centers
Harvard Graduate School of Education
336 Gutman Library
Cambridge, MA 02138
617-495-9812

PART II

PROCESSES FOR BUILDING A LEARNING COMMUNITY

CHAPTER 6

COLLABORATION

PROBLEM SCENARIO

As a principal, you want to initiate a collaborative process to convert your school into a learning community with a clear vision. You are replacing a principal who had an authoritative decision-making style. The school's staff members have heard the buzzword collaboration, but they have little faith in the concept because of their experiences with your predecessor. What does a collaborative process for forming a learning community with a clear vision mean for you as the new principal?

COLLABORATIVE PROCESS

Developing a learning community requires employing methods that encourage the joint efforts of teachers, administrators, staff, students, parents, and other members of the community. A learning community cannot function in isolation, the norm for many schools. Collaboration within a learning community means people working together, breaking down the walls of isolation built by solitary efforts of individuals inside and outside the school. The larger community must be invited to participate on a regular basis with a clear focus on improving student learning.

It is not an easy task to develop a collective spirit within the school learning community that honors the collaborative efforts of teachers, staff members, parents, and others in the community. Many aspects of the current structure of schools work against collaboration. Developing such a spirit is often a difficult process that can take years of work and meticulous development of relationships.

McDonald (1996) in *Redesigning School* emphasizes the difficulty of transforming the organizational context of learning from direct instruction in isolated classrooms to the community of learners. It is the exception, not the rule, for a school to have a culture of collaborative sharing about students, curriculum, instructional and assessment practices, or other critical educational issues. Schools must discard the common practices that isolate elements of the learning community into discrete cells (McDonald 1996). A principal endeavoring to create a community of learners must provide support, motivation, and encouragement as key parts of the collaborative process.

The collaborative process of a learning community is interwoven, ongoing, and nonlinear. Figure 6.1 shows the key elements, which are discussed in detail in this chapter.

DEVELOPING COLLEGIALITY

The principal, teachers, and other staff members must join together as colleagues, rather than work in isolation, if a school is to become a learning community focused on students' learning. The congenial relationships existing in most schools can help build collegiality. Barth (1990) points out that collegiality should not be confused with congeniality. Congeniality refers to the friendliness people manifest in social settings such as chitchat about a weekend trip, a ballgame, or a new recipe. In contrast, collegiality entails high levels of collaboration among members of a group, such as a school's principal, teachers, and staff members. It is characterized by mutual respect, shared work values, cooperation, and specific conversations about teaching and learning (Sergiovanni 1995). A principal who expects to break a school's isolation and move the staff members beyond congeniality must constantly foster collegiality.

Little (1981, 28) defines **collegiality** in a school as having four specific behaviors:

- Adults in schools talk about practice. These conversations about teaching and learning are frequent, continuous, concrete, and precise.

FIGURE 6.1
Elements of the Col-
laborative Process

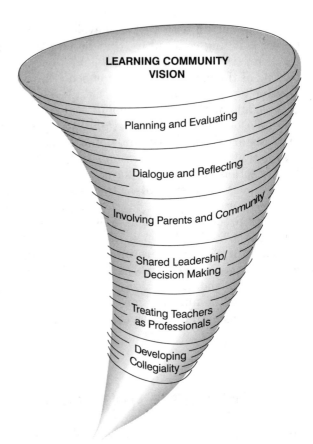

- Adults in schools observe each other engaged in the practice of teaching and administration. These observations
  become the practice to reflect on and talk about.
- Adults engage together in work on curriculum by planning, designing, researching, and evaluating curriculum.
- Adults in schools teach each other what they know about
  teaching, learning, and leading. Craft knowledge about
  teaching and learning are revealed, articulated, and
  shared. There is a constant atmosphere of interaction
  among staff about teaching and learning.

The principal's job of fostering collegial relationships in a school is
made more difficult by the history of schooling as the isolated work of
individual teachers in their classrooms and the principal's traditional
role as sole authority and decision-maker. Joyce, Wolf, and Calhoun
(1993) comment on the importance of collaboration and collegiality:

The norms of isolation and extreme autonomy that characterized schooling, (Lortie 1975; Little 1990; and Rosenholtz 1989) the friction and confusion between levels of the organization, and the fragmentation of initiatives are increasingly understood as unhealthy . . . research is gradually establishing a clear connection between the mental health of the organization and the people in it and the growth of students. Integrated organizations, with collaborative social climates, are more healthy to work in and generate more job satisfaction across roles.[1]

It is incumbent upon a principal to serve as a role model for collegiality and foster such relationships among teachers and staff members through a clear focus on student learning. The principal must first become a colleague and clearly communicate to all staff members the improvements that collegiality can bring to the school. Principals who have planted the seeds of collegiality must make it grow by reinforcing its importance daily in discussions with teachers and other staff members and by exhibiting it in daily actions. Through these practices collegiality will become the school's expected norm.

REFLECTIONS: GIVEN WHAT YOU KNOW ABOUT THE IMPORTANCE

OF COLLEGIALITY IN TRANSFORMING A SCHOOL INTO A LEARN-

ING COMMUNITY, HOW WOULD YOU AS PRINCIPAL FOSTER COL-

LEGIALITY? WHAT COULD YOU DO AS A PRINCIPAL TO INSTILL

THIS QUALITY? WRITE DOWN YOUR THOUGHTS.

Little's 1981 research (cited in Barth 1990) found that norms of collegiality were developed when principals clearly:

- Communicated their expectations for teacher cooperation.
- Provided a model for collegiality by working firsthand with teachers in improving the school.
- Rewarded expressions of collegiality among teachers by providing recognition, release time, money, and other support resources.
- Protected teachers who were willing to go against expected norms of privatism and isolation by engaging in collegial behaviors. (p. 33)

---

[1] Reprinted with permission of Association for Supervision and Curriculum Development from *The Self-Renewing School*, 25, by Bruce Joyce, James Wolf, and Emily Calhoun. © 1993 by Association for Supervision and Curriculum Development.

A principal who is committed to developing a school learning community must recognize that fostering collegiality will be difficult, long-term work.

Barth (1990) discusses the importance of collegiality for a school to become a community of learners.

> I think that the problem of how to change things from "I" to "we," of how to bring a good measure of collegiality and relatedness to adults who work in schools, is one that belongs on the national agenda of school improvement—at the top. It belongs at the top because the relationships among adults in schools are the basis, the precondition, the sine qua non that allow, energize, and sustain all other attempts at school improvement. Unless adults talk with one another, very little will change.[2]

It is the relationships and quality of discussions about learning and the learner that are important if a school is to become a learning community. There is growing evidence that when principals value collegiality, schools do improve, gaining through relationships of respect among teachers and administrators who then are more willing and apt to engage in meaningful discussions about how to improve education.

As the leader of the school, the principal must keep constantly focused on student learning and the progress of the school as a whole. The difficult tasks of leading school change and developing a collaborative process and collegiality make up the working atmosphere of a learning community. The principal must constantly assess through leadership opportunities the development of a collaborative school culture. School cultures that turn into learning communities do so slowly as the principal encourages the process by providing time for people to gather and discuss ideas and experiences and facilitates other types of interaction that can eventually result in collegial relationships.

Strong leadership by principals seems to be essential because of their broad responsibility for overseeing the health of their schools, making and coordinating initiatives, and generating a democratic framework and process that binds the organization (Joyce, Wolf, and Calhoun 1993). The principal cannot just follow established routines for getting things done but instead must act as a problem-solver by helping diagnose problems, generating the impetus for solutions, and implementing solutions. The principal as leader can crystallize a problem and has the capability within the school community to create collective solutions through a collaborative process.

---

[2] Reprinted with permission of Jossey-Bass Inc. from *Improving Schools from Within,* 32, by Roland Barth. © 1990 by Jossey-Bass Inc., Publishers.

PROCESS FOR BUILDING A COLLEGIAL CULTURE

It is clear from reviews of the literature on successful schools that building a culture that promotes and sustains a school's concept of success is key. According to Norris (cited in Hughes 1994), a school's culture is a representation of what its members collectively believe themselves to be; it is their self-concept. It reflects what they value and what they tell others they believe is important. Just as an individual's self-concept shapes one's personality, so does an organization's perception of itself determine what it ultimately becomes. Thus, creating a collegial culture within a learning community includes the following interactive and critical elements: mutual respect, essential conversations about teaching and learning, shared values and vision, clear expectations, time to share, teamwork, professional development, inquiry, and reflective practice (see Figure 6.2).

Colleagues must have mutual respect for each other and their work. This can develop within a learning community through time together, professional development, and activities that require cooperation and teamwork. Ongoing professional development, reflecting on current practices, and having meaningful discussions about teaching and learning allow collegiality to develop and grow within a school.

FIGURE 6.2
Process of Building
a Collegial Culture

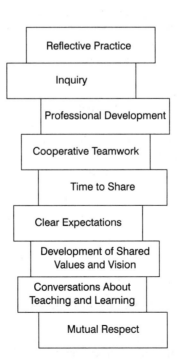

Through this process of collegial culture-building, a principal and staff can transform a school population from a collection of "I"s to a learning community of "We"s. Culture building is an essential leadership ability of a principal (Deal and Peterson 1990). Saphier and King (1985) point out:

> Cultures are built through the everyday business of school life. It is the way business is handled that both forms and reflects the culture.... Culture building occurs ... through the way people use educational, human and technical skills in handling daily events or establishing regular practices. (p. 72)

School culture reflects the shared values, beliefs, and commitments of school members about the school and the process of schooling. Sergiovanni (1991) puts it this way:

> What the school stands for and believes about education, organization, and human relationships; what the school seeks to accomplish; its essential elements and features; and the image it seeks to project are the deep-rooted defining characteristics shaping the substance of its culture. (p. 218)

The very essence of the living collective vision of schooling is projected by a school's culture. The school culture permeates what people think and what they do in schools. Schein (1985) sees culture in schools as the basic assumptions and beliefs shared by members of an organization, which operate on a subconscious level, defining the organization's view of itself and its environment. Many schools become trapped within a long-existing culture that does not meet the needs of the current school community. This can be seen in the many schools that have not adapted to the needs of their changing, demographically diverse student populations. The principal and staff members must examine the school's culture and how to work with it, for only with a clear knowledge of that culture can they bring about change and make a commitment to developing a collegial culture. Collegiality as a cultural norm is essential if a school wishes to establish a true learning community dedicated to a continuing process of improvement and renewal.

TREATING TEACHERS AS PROFESSIONALS

As professional educators, teachers work with the principal to improve the school's teaching and learning practices. A principal, as leader of a learning community, must base all actions on the premise that all teachers are professionals and treat them as such. Sustaining this professional attitude and creating a culture of collegiality are crucial in the collaborative process for establishing trust, respect, and reflection within the learning community.

Rosenholtz and Kyle (1984), in "Teacher Isolation," describe the classic elements of professionalism that demonstrate the centrality of the collaborative ethic for a learning community:

1. Professionals share technical knowledge that is developed through professional training. When teachers share experiences through problem solving, they build a body of professional knowledge that stands apart from the lay person's knowledge. Just as attorneys and physicians have specialized knowledge and a technical language to transmit that knowledge, so, too, do teachers in collaborative settings.

2. Professionals determine what and how work is to be done and the goals of the work. Similar goals afford teachers a reason to share ideas about how success is to be measured. . . . In short professionals control their work and the standards for that work.

3. Finally, professionals supervise, review and evaluate their own colleagues with a view toward quality control. A professional protocol of live and let live, in which teachers are left adrift to survive primarily by their own wits, invites scrutiny by outsiders whenever quality appears to decline. Professionals police themselves in order to maintain control over the work that they do and the manner in which it is done. (p. 15)

Teacher professionalism is the expected norm within schools but is too rarely practiced. Its absence deletes a critical element from the development of a working, collegial learning community. A principal must foster and provide opportunities for teachers to discuss and adopt professionalism as a cultural norm.

SHARED LEADERSHIP/ DECISION MAKING

Within the school learning community, the principal must empower teachers and staff members to lead and share in decision making to develop curriculum, instruction, and assessment. Kruse, Louis, and Bryk (1994) state:

Strong professional communities show high levels of teacher autonomy. Researchers suggest that teachers with more discretion regarding their work feel more responsible for how well their students learn. The flexibility allows them to respond to specific needs they see. Instead of being guided by rules, they are guided by the norms and beliefs of the professional community. (p. 5)

The empowerment of teachers by the principal and by themselves is vital if teachers are to truly become full members of a school learning community. If individual teachers see themselves as important participants and leaders, it will become apparent through their efforts. Research by McLaughlin and Talbert (1992) shows that teachers in professional communities with cohesive, highly collegial environments report high levels of innovation, energy and enthusiasm, and support for personal growth and learning. Teachers who belong to communities of this sort also report strong commitment to teaching and to all the students with whom they work. Fullan (1993) emphasizes the importance of empowering teachers:

The challenge is to improve education in the only way it can be, through the day-to-day actions of empowered individuals. (p. 70)

The role of the principal becomes one of capacity-building for the school learning community by helping teachers make decisions for themselves and establish responsibility and accountability for their actions. Working together for causes they believe in requires teachers and the principal to sacrifice their own needs and join together to improve student learning. Prawat (1993) states that learning communities thrive on commitment and make decisions together as events unfold.

Senge's (1990) new view of leadership in a learning organization centers on leaders as designers, stewards, and teachers. The principal, as one of the leaders within a learning organization, is responsible for helping members of that organization continually expand their capabilities to shape their future—that is, leaders are responsible for learning. Shared leadership and decision making provide principals and teachers with rich learning experiences to guide the development of the learning community. Designing learning processes where people can work together, acting as a steward to facilitate and seek a broader purpose and direction for the school, and acting as a teacher who fosters learning for everyone are important roles that Senge (1990) emphasizes for the learning organization leader. It is these important roles in a school that the principal must carry out if a learning community is to function, be nurtured, and grow.

INVOLVING PARENTS AND COMMUNITY

Principals must invite parent and others in the community to become partners in the learning process at school, at home, and in the community. Parents, a child's first and primary teachers, can reinforce the work of the school learning community both while the child is in school and when the child is at home or in the community. To better do its job, a school must welcome, involve, and provide training for parents, who want the best education for their children and can benefit from that learning and training.

Parental involvement must be meaningful, going beyond class parties, bake sales, and PTA or club meetings. It calls for real involvement with the students' learning both in the classroom and at home. Sharpening and adding to parents' teaching skills and helping them gain insight into the learning process can draw these important figures into the school learning community. Giving a parent a role to play in schooling can enrich the learning experience of both parent and child.

Glickman (1993) gives some insights into the importance of parental and community involvement:

> A school, with its charter, has involved parents and community members in decision making. It has developed a covenant of learning principles and, through critical study, it has sampled additional parental and community responses to proposed actions. Those parents and community members who get involved typically become strong advocates of change and help school personnel inform the larger community. People involved in the process tend to reason more than those who are not involved about benefits for all children.[3]

The entire community benefits from education. Community involvement provides the school learning community with rich resources of expertise, experience, application, and opportunities for community service. Principals and teachers must understand the importance of community involvement and decide how to connect the school learning community with the larger community surrounding the school. Individually, the principal can meet with various representatives of the community including the Chamber of Commerce, city and county government, service clubs (for example, Rotary, Lions, Kiwanis), citizens' groups, churches, businesses, and other groups that

---

[3] Reprinted with permission of Jossey-Bass Inc. from *Renewing America's Schools: A Guide for School-Based Action*, 105, by Carl Glickman. © 1993 by Jossey-Bass Inc., Publishers.

represent the diversity of the community. The principal along with faculty and staff members can take the initiative in providing opportunities for the community to become involved in the school learning community. Further, the principal should encourage teachers and staff members to find a variety of ways to make connections to the surrounding community.

Making these important links can help the school learning community expand into the surrounding community. Students, teachers, and staff can integrate learning activities with community endeavors and make learning productive for the larger community. Community involvement requires actual work, allowing students to see the results of their learning and efforts in the community. This interconnection of the school and the community can draw students, teachers, and schools closer to the community to the betterment of both.

Community involvement will provide a vital link between the school learning community and the larger world and its reality. Learning communities cannot exist in isolation. The walls of the school and the classroom must open to the community and the world, now more than ever a global village. Preparation for citizenship in the twenty-first century demands that students involve themselves in their community rather than just passively listening to lectures about it in the classroom.

REFLECTIONS: AS A PROSPECTIVE PRINCIPAL, LOOK AROUND

YOUR SCHOOL. HOW INVOLVED IN THE COMMUNITY ARE THE

STUDENTS AND TEACHERS? IS IT A TOKEN EFFORT, OR HAS THE

COMMUNITY BEEN INTERWOVEN IN THE FABRIC OF CLASSROOM

LEARNING? TAKE SOME TIME TO WRITE DOWN YOUR THOUGHTS.

PLANNING, REFLECTING, AND EVALUATING

Teachers and principals should collaboratively plan, reflect, and evaluate the practices and progress the learning community is making with regard to learning for students and themselves. Through the planning process teachers can share their collective knowledge about aspects of the curriculum and the instruction strategies to produce the optimum learning experience for the students while they strengthen their professional relationships. The mutual support and respect that teachers and the principal give each other as they work together is fundamental to fostering collegiality.

Continual reflection on practice by teachers through meaningful discussions of teaching and learning—as well as frequent peer observation and coaching sessions—provides for an ongoing dialogue within the learning community. The principal needs to nurture this process by providing time and encouraging these reflective practices. As colleagues, teachers and principals should discuss questions about the why, what, and how of curriculum, instruction, and assessment every day.

Lieberman (1995) emphasizes the importance of reflective practice in a learning community:

> Transforming schools into learning organizations, in which people work together to solve problems collectively, is more than a question of inserting a new curriculum or a new program. It also involves thinking through how the content and processes of learning can be redefined in ways that engage students and teachers in the active pursuit of learning goals; it involves a joining of experiential learning and content knowledge. Teaching as telling, the model that has dominated pedagogy and the consequent organization of schooling to date, is being called into question as professional learning for teachers increasingly connects to this reconsidered view of schools. (p. 592)

Resnick (1987) and Schon (1991) state that learning and organizational theorists have found that people learn best through active involvement and through thinking about and becoming articulate about what they have learned and then reflecting on practice. Lieberman (1995) sees this as an expanded view of professional learning, both personal and professional, both individual and collective, both inquiry-based and technical.

Lieberman (1995) concludes:

> If reform plans are to be made operational—thus enabling teachers to really change the way they work—then teachers must have opportunities to discuss, think about, try out, and hone new practices. This means that they must be involved in learning about, developing, and using new ideas with their students. They can do this in a number of ways:
>
> ▪ by building new roles (e.g., teachers leader, peer coach, teacher researcher);
>
> ▪ by creating new structures (e.g., problem-solving groups, decision-making teams);

■ by working on new tasks (e.g., journal and proposal writing, learning about assessment, creating standards, analyzing or writing case studies of practice; and

■ by creating a culture of inquiry, wherein professional learning is expected, sought after, and an ongoing part of teaching and school life. (p. 593)

Engaging in meaningful conversations about learning and teaching with teachers will help the principal join in the continual dialogue within the school learning community. Involvement, not separation, is key to the principal's role as the school learning community pursues new methods to boost student learning. The ability to ask good questions and to listen intently before voicing an opinion will help the principal develop and hold together a learning community.

Resources and time to share are important means by which a principal can support teachers' work. The principal has the primary responsibility for providing the resources (money, time, personnel, and materials) necessary for a school faculty to implement new practices and programs. It is the utilization of various resources for school improvement that a principal can leverage for change. By providing faculty members with books for reading, literary supplemental materials, professional development activities, and release time to visit and peer coach one another, the principal enables teachers to adopt and institutionalize new instructional and curricular practices in early literacy. Offering adequate resources and time to meet as individuals or in groups, attend professional development activities, and discuss progress and concerns with one another and the principal demonstrates a significant commitment on the part of the principal and the school working together.

Shared decision making in all aspects of the school will send the message that the principal seriously seeks the participation and involvement of teachers, students, and parents. Evaluating processes such as reviewing programs, materials, and use of budgets should also reflect the participation of all members of the school learning community: teachers, students, parents, and the community.

Darling-Hammond (1995), in "Policies That Support Professional Development in an Era of Reform," reinforces the need for principals to rethink practices:

To fulfill these new roles and expectations for leadership, however, administrators need to understand what the conception of teaching and learning that motivate the nation's reform agenda look like in classrooms and how these visions of practice relate to teachers' opportunities to learn. Administrators, no less than teachers, urgently need the chance to rethink practice and to learn the new perspectives and skills that are consistent with reformers' visions of teaching and learning for understanding. (p. 603)

COMMON VISION

Finally, the school learning community must establish a common vision based on the other elements of the collaborative process: fostering collegiality, shared leadership and decision making, teacher professionalism, planning, reflecting, and evaluating and parental and community involvement. This vision will develop as people in the school work together, formulating it from their varied beliefs about education and points of view.

It is important for the principal to have a clear vision of schooling to serve as the foundation for daily actions and long-range planning to improve the school's quality of life and learning. Vision is what separates the principals who are school leaders from those who are simply managers. Vision is the capacity to create and communicate a view of the desired state of affairs that induces commitment among those working in the organization (Sergiovanni 1995, 90). Teachers, staff, students, parents, and the community can see the principal's vision—or lack of it—articulated each day in the principal's actions.

Numerous studies show that effective leaders must have vision. Bennis (1984), in studies of business executives in highly successful organizations, found the key ingredient of leadership was **compelling vision**. Dwyer and others (1983) in studying principals found that all successful principals had a vision to guide their actions. A principal without vision is like a ship without a rudder lost in the sea of schooling.

Barth (1990) summarizes thoughts on the importance of vision:

> The personal vision of school practitioners is a kind of moral imagination that gives them the ability to see schools not as they are, but as they would like them to become. I find practitioners' personal visions usually deeply submerged, sometimes fragmentary and seldom articulated. A painful pause usually awaits anyone who asks a teacher or principal, "What is your vision for a good school?" But I am convinced the vision is there. I find that it usually emerges when schoolpeople complete sentences like: "When I leave this school I would like to be remembered for . . . "; "I want my school to become a place where . . . "; or "The kind of school I would like my own children to attend would . . . "[4]

---

[4] Reprinted with permission of Jossey-Bass Inc. from *Improving Schools from Within,* 148, by Roland Barth. © 1990 by Jossey-Bass Inc., Publishers.

Answering the following questions can help principals clarify their vision of schooling:

What is the purpose of schooling?

What does a successful school learning community look like?

What should students know and be able to do?

What kinds of learning experiences should students have?

How is learning assessed?

How does school transformation or change take place?

Who is responsible for ensuring that the school delivers the desired results of success for all students?

How is a school learning community developed?

The **vision thing** is a key concept of successful leadership for the principalship. A principal whose daily actions are not linked to an overall dream of what the school could be is a mere manager, doomed to fall short of the leadership that can elevate a school to the higher state of learning community. As Barth (1990) writes:

> A personal vision, then, is one's overall conception of what the educator wants the organization to stand for; what its primary mission is; what its basic, core values are; a sense of how all the parts fit together; and, above all, how the vision maker fits into the grand plan. (p. 148)

Thus, for the learning community to develop a working, collective school vision, the principal must have a personal vision as a leader of the school.

AN EXAMPLE OF A PRINCIPAL'S VISION

Describing her vision of schooling, elementary school principal Cynthia Cooksey (1995) wrote:

> I believe all students at every level should experience a positive school culture and climate which reflects a strong student-centered educational philosophy. Student-centered factors that enable students to create their own meaning from curriculum will include:
>
> ■ a variety of active experiences which focus attention and challenge their thinking.
>
> ■ putting thoughts into words, both orally and written, in order to organize and to clarify their thinking.

- using real-life experiences and primary source materials which connect to their everyday life.

- creating real, authentic products.

- putting together complex concepts and applying skills across subject matter boundaries.

- weighing personal and/or group values and norms against the ethical implications of what they are learning.

- allowing students to be more independent, involved in their education, and to be responsible for their own behavior.

What I envision as the mission for schooling in the East Palo Alto/Menlo Park community is to:

- help students see the "big" world, feel worthy of claiming a part of it as a goal, develop values, attitudes, and habits consistent with the goal, and see classroom work as relevant goals set for themselves.

- teach students to use computer-based technologies for processing information, communicating with others, and creating works of self-expression.

- provide students with the ability to be comfortable in various groups of people.

- help students develop skills in social interactions characterized by concern, tolerance, and respect for others.

- provide encouragement and incentives for students to pursue academic and occupational goals irrespective of primary language and ethnic background.

- convince students of their essential worth and provide students with recognition of the dignity and work of each person.

- help students of color understand that racism is a global system, and help them accept themselves.

- prepare students to control, define, and manage their own socioeconomic development.

- free students of color from the psychological dependence on others; it must teach them to think and act on their own. Education must become a process that educates for liberation and survival.

I am committed to providing opportunities which assist the students in making self-directed, realistic, and responsible decisions when solving problems that may confront them in our multicultural, ever-changing world. Ultimately, schooling is a process of living and not preparation for future living. (pp. 3–4)

FIGURE 6.3
Establishing a Collective Vision

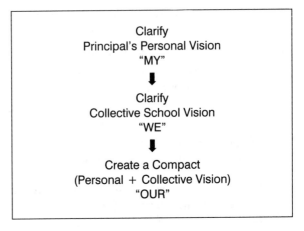

ESTABLISHING A COLLECTIVE VISION: A COMPACT

How does a principal take a personal vision and help originate an overall school vision that springs from and belongs to the entire school community? First, the principal must ensure that all the school's stakeholders—teachers, staff, students, parents, and the entire community—join together in formulating a vision of the school that reflects their hopes and dreams, interests and needs, and values and beliefs about schooling. The learning community can set forth a collective vision of what the school should be in a compact expressing their common beliefs about what the school stands for.

Creating a compact that embodies the school's vision requires the principal to broaden the personal vision ("my" vision) into a collective vision ("our" vision) for the school (see Figure 6.3). Through the development of a compact, members of a learning community articulate their community's beliefs. Each member of the school learning community should sign the compact as a symbol of commitment to the vision and to a sense of obligation on the part of each individual to make the vision a reality.

Often in today's schools the principal, teachers, student, and staff members carry out their daily work without a real understanding of what their school stands for or has committed itself to doing. Establishing a compact can prompt members of the school to commit to a set of beliefs and reinforce their commitment to strive to carry out the compact's goals. Signing the compact makes a very powerful statement for members of the school learning community and provides the foundation for actions within the school. The following two compacts created by schools are provided as samples.

SAMPLE COMPACTS

Figures 6.4 and 6.5 illustrate two sample compacts that were created and signed by schools. Each compact demonstrates the school's indi-

---

East Side High School
COMPACT

We commit ourselves to the following beliefs:

1. We believe all students are capable learners who can experience success in an academic setting in our high schools. We recognize the need to place emphasis on ninth and tenth grade Latino and African American students not meeting academic expectations.

2. We believe professional educators should make decisions regarding curriculum, instruction, and evaluation based on verifiable research and effective practice.

3. We believe a collaborative community of professional educators and support staff is a vital component in the continuing process of improving the quality of life and learning for students and adults within our schools.

Signatures of all members

FIGURE 6.4
One Example of a Sample Compact

vidual beliefs and commitment to the beliefs by signatures of all school learning community members.

The personal commitment of all parties in the school community to the school compact provides the energy and enthusiasm needed to carry out the beliefs. Without commitment there is no strength to uphold the compact or school vision statement, leaving its laudable goals to languish as mere words on paper. The desired comment can be cemented by having all members of a learning community sign the compact. This becomes a public statement of commitment heard by all members of the outside community. This is confirmed by Sergiovanni's (1995) statement:

> When both vision and covenant (like a compact) are present, teachers and students respond with increased motivation and commitment and their performance is beyond expectations. The affirming of values that accompanies purposing is a motivational force far more powerful than the bureaucratic and psychological transactions that characterize leadership by bartering and building. They become the very basis upon which we construct our reality and from which we derive sense and meaning. (pp. 132–33)

The members of the learning community must revisit their commitment to the compact and the vision of the school regularly; otherwise their actions and attitudes and the school culture may not reflect their stated beliefs. The principal as leader of the school learning com-

---

El Roble Elementary School
COMPACT

As involved, committed, and open-minded professional educators who intend to bring about change, we dedicate ourselves to the following:

- Through collaboration, communication, and mutual respect, we will become a resilient community of educators, promoting high expectations and active involvement in learning for students and adults within our school.

- We will respect each other and the diversity of the school community.

- We will provide an environment in which everyone has a sense of belonging and where positive self-esteem is promoted.

- All students can learn and become lifelong learners and productive citizens.

- To help students engage and maintain interest in quality education, there will be a variety of opportunities and resources for academic, personal, and social development within the school community.

- Through consensus, we will make informed decisions regarding curriculum, instruction, evaluation, professional development, resources, and policies effecting El Roble.

Signatures of all members

FIGURE 6.5
Another Sample Compact

munity must keep the commitment to the compact continually in focus as decisions and plans are made within the school.

Finally, it is important to remember that in recent studies of school improvement initiatives where substantial student learning occurred, school staff members kept the interests of students as learners central throughout the planning, implementation, and assessment phases and worked together with a common vision (Joyce, Wolf, and Calhoun 1993).

SUMMARY

In building a learning community, the principal must use a collaborative process that encourages interaction and connections among teachers, students, parents, and the rest of the community as they develop a common vision for the school. The elements of the collaborative process, including collegiality, shared leadership and decision making, planning, reflecting, and evaluating, and the involvement of parents and the community are crucial to developing a learning community. Teachers must be treated as empowered professionals who can make daily decisions to improve learning for students.

Building a school learning community is difficult and time-consuming work. It starts with the principal's personal vision about schooling and develops into a collective vision for the school community through a defined compact and the commitment to action by the principal, students, teachers, staff members, and the rest of the community.

REFLECTIVE ACTIVITIES

1. Collaborative Process for a School Learning Community

What are the collaborative processes you see occurring in your school or district? How would you define your ideal school collaborative process? Discuss in class.

2. Interview Several Teachers About the Collaborative Process

Interview several teachers at different schools regarding their involvement in their schools. What key points did you learn about what teachers think about their school involvement and about the collaborative process?

3. Parents and Community in the Collaborative Process

What are schools in your area doing to involve parents and the community in a collaborative process for school improvement? Research several schools and discuss what you learned in class.

4. A Principal's Vision

The vision you hold as principal for your school is crucial. What are your deeply held beliefs about schooling (quality of life and learning) and how do they affect your actions? Write your vision of schooling and how you, as a principal, would express it to your school.

5. Developing a School Compact

How would you develop a school compact that would be signed by members of the school community? What would be the key elements of your ideal school compact?

SUGGESTED READINGS

Barth, Roland. 1990. *Improving Schools from Within*. San Francisco: Jossey-Bass.

Glickman, Carl. 1993. *Renewing America's Schools: A Guide for School-Based Action*. San Francisco: Jossey-Bass.

Joyce, Bruce, James Wolf, and Emily Calhoun. 1993. *The Self-Renewing School*. Alexandria, VA: Association for Supervision and Curriculum Development.

Kruse, Sharon, Karen Seashore Louis, and Anthony Bryk. 1994. "Building a Professional Community in Schools," *Brief*, Spring 1994, Madison, WI: Center on Organization and Restructuring of Schools, University of Wisconsin.

McDonald, Joseph P. 1996. *Redesigning School: Lessons for the 21st Century*. San Francisco: Jossey-Bass.

REFERENCES

Barth, Roland. 1990. *Improving Schools from Within*. San Francisco: Jossey-Bass.

Bennis, Warren. 1984. Transformational Power and Leadership. In *Leadership and Organizational Culture*, edited by Thomas J. Sergiovanni and John E. Corbally, 64–71. Urbana-Champaign, IL: University of Illinois Press.

Cooksey, Cynthia. 1995. Unpublished paper. "Essential Questions About Schooling—Response" by Cynthia Cooksey, principal of James Flood School, East Palo Alto, CA: Ravenswood Union School District.

Darling-Hammond, Linda. 1995. Policies That Support Professional Development in an Era of Reform. *Phi Delta Kappan* 76(8): 597–604.

Deal, Terrence E., and Kent D. Peterson. 1990. *The Principal's Role in Shaping School Culture*. Washington, DC: Office of Educational Research and Improvement. ED 3256 914.

Dwyer, David, Ginny Lee, Brian Rowan, and Steven Bassert. 1983. *Five Principles in Action: Perspectives on Instructional Management*. San Francisco: Far West Laboratory for Educational Research and Development.

Fullan, Michael. 1993. *Change Forces: Probing the Depths of Educational Reform*. New York: Falmer Press.

Glickman, Carl. 1993. *Renewing America's Schools: A Guide for School-Based Action*. San Francisco: Jossey-Bass.

Hughes, Larry W., ed. 1994. *The Principal As Leader*. Upper Saddle River, NJ: Merrill/Prentice Hall.

Joyce, Bruce, James Wolf, and Emily Calhoun. 1993. *The Self-Renewing School*. Alexandria, VA: Association for Supervision and Curriculum Development.

Kruse, Sharon, Karen Seashore Louis, and Anthony Bryk. 1994. "Building a Professional Community in Schools," *Brief*, Spring 1994, Madison, WI: Center on Organization and Restructuring of Schools, University of Wisconsin.

Lieberman, Ann. 1995. Practices That Support Teacher Development: Transforming Conceptions of Professional Learning. *Phi Delta Kappan* 76(8): 591–96.

Little, Judith. 1981. *School Success and Staff Development in Urban Desegregated Schools*. Boulder, CO: Center for Action Research.

Little, Judith. 1990. The Persistence of Privacy: Autonomy and Initiative in Teachers' Professional Relations. *Teachers College Record* 91(4): 509–36.

Lortie, Daniel. 1975. *School Teacher*. Chicago: University of Chicago Press.

McDonald, Joseph P. 1996. *Redesigning School: Lessons for the 21st Century*. San Francisco: Jossey-Bass.

McLaughlin, Milbrey W., and Joan E. Talbert. 1992. *Social Constructions of Students: Challenges to Policy Coherence*, 92–147. Palo Alto, CA: Stanford University, Center for Research on the Context of Secondary Teaching.

Prawat, Richard. 1993. The Role of the Principal in the Development of Learning Communities. *Wingspan: The Pedamorphosis Communique* 9(2): 7–9.

Resnick, Lauren. 1987. "AERA Presidential Address." Paper delivered at the annual meeting of the American Educational Research Association, Washington, D.C., 1987.

Rosenholtz, Susan. 1989. *Teacher's Workplace: The Social Organization of Schools*. White Plains, NY: Longman.

Rosenholtz, Susan J., and Susan J. Kyle. Teacher Isolation: Barrier to Professionalism. *American Educator*, Winter 1984.

Saphier, Jon, and Matthew King. 1985. Good Seeds Grow in Strong Cultures. *Educational Leadership* 42(6): 67–74.

Schein, Edgar. 1985. *Organizational Culture and Leadership*. San Francisco: Jossey-Bass.

Schon, Donald, ed. 1991. *The Reflective Turn: Case Studies in and on Educational Practice*. New York: Teachers College Press.

Senge, Peter. 1990. *The Fifth Discipline: The Art and Practice of the Learning Organization*. New York: Doubleday.

Sergiovanni, Thomas J. 1991. *The Principalship: A Reflective Practice Perspective*. 2d ed. Boston: Allyn and Bacon.

Sergiovanni, Thomas J. 1995. *The Principalship: A Reflective Practice Perspective*. 3d ed. Boston: Allyn and Bacon.

CHAPTER 7

FACILITATION OF CURRICULUM, INSTRUCTION, AND ASSESSMENT

PROBLEM SCENARIO

As a principal, you must work with teachers, staff, the district, parents, and other community members to provide a program of curriculum, instruction, and assessment that leads to successful learning experiences for students. What issues will you face as you review the existing curriculum, instruction, and assessment in your school to lead to improvement? What processes will you use to evaluate the current program? Who will be involved, and what is the principal's role?

PRINCIPAL'S FACILITATIVE ROLE

Curriculum, instruction, and assessment are at the heart of creating and sustaining a learning community where the act of teaching all students how to learn, think, and solve problems is central to the real work of the school. This chapter focuses on the principal's role in facilitating the development of curriculum content, instructional practices, and methods of assessment that will meet the needs of all the school's students.

Recent studies (Murphy 1994; Leithwood 1992) on school restructuring clarify the evolution of the principalship from manager to instructional leader to the current role of facilitator-leader. Cordeiro (1994) describes the principal's role in today's school learning community as that of a generalist who, through collaboration, distributes and coordinates leadership opportunities that focus on curriculum, instruction, and assessment. The facilitative and collaborative work of the principal provides continuous opportunities for generative learning and improved professional practices within the school. The principal is no longer the sole instructional leader, but one who facilitates instructional leadership within the school by allowing teachers to use their instructional expertise and enjoy the opportunity to share in leadership.

Thus, over the last several decades the role of the principal has changed with regard to instructional leadership. The central focus on the principal as instructional leader for the school, which developed during the educational reform movement of the 1980s, has seen a continual evolution in the school restructuring movement in the 1990s. In a synthesis of studies on the impact of school restructuring efforts, Murphy (1994, 20–53) describes four new patterns in the principal's role:

- Principal led from center rather than the top (led from the center of a network of human relationships, rather than from the top of an organizational pyramid).
- Principal enabled and supported teacher success.
- Principal managed a constellation of change efforts.
- Principal extended the school community.

The role of instructional leader has changed from being the sole province of the principal to one of shared leadership with teachers. Murphy's (1994) findings reveal that principals in restructuring schools engaged in substantial delegation of leadership responsibilities by yielding power and decision-making authority to teachers. Odden (1995) states that the new role of the principal in instructional leadership is facilitative:

> Rather than being the key decision-maker and "thinker" in the school as the person holding the top position in the hierarchy, principals in restructuring schools facilitated the activities of myriad groups and subgroups all engaged in decision-making on several fronts. (p. 190)

As it develops, a school learning community moves away from the bureaucratic structure of top-down authority toward consensus and responsibility for instructional leadership as an ongoing collaborative process among teachers and principal (Goldring and Rallis 1993; Murphy and Hallinger 1993).

To make this delegation of leadership work, the principal must develop numerous processes and mechanisms for collaborative decision making. The principal's role is not to be the leader of all groups but to orchestrate the effective and substantive functioning of groups. The principal uses collaborative processes to participate not as the chair of the group or the most active or most knowledgeable member but as a facilitator. Thus, the principal allows teachers to assume instructional leadership and decision-making roles. The more teachers participate, provide leadership, and learn, the more their leadership and collaborative abilities will expand. Teachers must feel empowerment and support from the principal if they are to take an active role in developing curriculum, instruction, and assessments that help all students succeed.

In facilitating the instructional leadership in teachers, the principal must enable and support the teachers within the school. Principals need to work with teachers in these new instructional leadership roles through the development of a common vision and compact for the school, as discussed in Chapter 6. According to Murphy (1994), Cordeiro (1994), and Odden (1995), the principal must cultivate the development of the collaborative decision-making process where teachers work together with access to information and resources critical to effective instructional decision making and promote substantial professional development to implement new curriculum and instructional practices. Teachers need to know that they have the power, information, resources, and support to build their school learning community. The principal as facilitator must reinforce the message of shared instructional leadership for improving curriculum, instruction, and assessment. The principal must empower the teachers to assume instructional leadership and provide the support for change. Murphy's (1994) summary of studies on restructuring schools substantiates the principal's diminished role in instructional leadership and simultaneously enhanced role of managing numerous activities and plans for school improvement.

Recent research (Beck and Murphy 1993; Greenfield 1987; Murphy 1990) on major curriculum change found that when teachers assumed key leadership roles, schools made more progress in implementing new, thinking-oriented curriculum. These studies also found that the effectiveness of these teacher roles depended on support and sustenance from the principal. This shift from instructional leader to reform facilitator and manager represents a major alteration in the assumed role for the principalship.

According to Beck and Murphy (1993), the phrases used to describe the principal's role have changed over the decades from descriptions that stress the importance of technical expertise, such as **instructional leader**, to those that emphasize human relations, such as **facilitator** or **transformational leader**. Leithwood (1992) proposes using the phrase **transformational leader** to describe the 1990s principal in a role that blends technical expertise with human relations. Prager (1993) concludes in a restructuring study that a blend of collegiality processes and focus on curriculum was important to advance the effectiveness of school restructuring efforts. Thus, the principal takes on the role of facilitator in the process of developing, implementing, and evaluating curriculum, instruction, and assessment. In this role the principal keeps the vision and focus central and helps others, especially teachers, lead various efforts.

Because of the shift away from the primary role as instructional leader at the school, the principal's role extends into the school community. Murphy (1994) found that principals in restructuring schools played an important role in extending the school community to broader communities. Principals need to work directly with agencies, boards, parents, local businesses, and other community resources to broaden the connection of the school to the larger community. This role presents many challenges to a principal because of enormous demands on time and energy, along with the uncertainty and the complexity of working with the larger community. As Odden (1995) states:

> "Community" in restructuring efforts seemed to connote a dramatically expanded notion of school community, and the principal is a key individual at the vortex of these new and sometimes complicated interactions. (p. 191)

The principal's role as instructional leader has thus evolved from the command-and-control style of a bureaucracy to the facilitative and behind-the-scenes leadership roles that work in a decentralized restructuring school. In this role the principal enables teachers, parents, and the rest of the community to assume leadership and decision-making roles to promote improved curriculum, instruction, and assessment for all students.

CURRICULUM DEVELOPMENT

As the principalship has moved to a more facilitative role, the principal must provide the information, resources, and opportunities for teachers to understand, review, decide, and develop or implement curriculum that will lead to learning for all students. The principal must be knowledgeable about the latest trends in a variety of curriculum areas. A school's curriculum development must involve teachers in leadership

FIGURE 7.1
Curriculum Develop-
ment Process

- Clarify curriculum need
- Review current curriculum
- Describe curriculum review process
- Identify participants in process (teachers, parents, community)
- Research and study state and national cur- riculum documents
- Make recommendations based on study and need
- Provide opportunity for community input
- Present recommendations for review
- Revise and review recommendations
- Adopt curriculum recommendations

roles, with the principal helping to coordinate activities, resources, and a clear focus for their work. As the curriculum is being developed, teachers must hear from students, parents, the district, and the rest of the community as well as have access to research and the current state and national curriculum documents. The principal must establish a collaborative, collegial process for members of the community to work together to develop a curriculum that reflects the needs of all members of the school learning community.

The curriculum development process outlined in Figure 7.1 shows the important steps in the development and review of a curriculum area, which the principal facilitates with the involvement of teachers, district office staff, parents, and other community members.

Recent curriculum development efforts center on the content of the school curriculum—the knowledge, skills, and competencies that students must learn. When preparing to facilitate the curriculum development process, the principal should review the key principles of recent national curriculum reform efforts of the 1990s (Brophy 1992, 3):

- A focus on in-depth study of fewer topics known as identifying the curriculum "big ideas."
- Curriculum as a common core for all students.
- Emphasis on thinking and problem-solving skill development for all children.
- Use of a strong knowledge base on how to teach thinking and problem solving in the content areas by teachers.

▧ Teaching all students thinking, analysis, communication, and team skills to help them become successful adults.

The core curriculum areas of which a principal must have a good working knowledge include English or language arts, mathematics, science, and history or social studies. For other important curriculum content areas such as the arts, foreign language, and vocational education, the principal must have some basic understanding of content and purpose. National professional content groups, such as the National Council of Teachers of Science, Mathematics, English, and Social Studies, can provide a principal with information and guidelines in curriculum content and standards. Established state curriculum frameworks or standards, such as those in California, Kentucky, and South Carolina, also provide examples of curriculum standards for principals to use in curriculum development and review processes. In reviewing these various professional curriculum reports, Lewis (1990) found common themes:

▧ Emphasis on thinking and problem-solving skills.

▧ Development of basic skills, facts, and knowledge in context by engaging students in problem solving, rather than isolation through direct instruction.

▧ Adding more content and substance in the elementary grades in all content areas, but especially in science and history.

▧ More rigorous curriculum content for all students. Remedial programs have been criticized for putting students at a disadvantage by repetitious, dull-content, instructional strategies that do not match learning styles.

▧ Integration of curricula. Proposals included reading and writing across subject areas; interdisciplinary teaching; even integration of separate content (biology, chemistry, and physics) within subject areas; and thematic units that required knowledge from two or more content areas.

▧ Incorporating ethical issues, controversial topics, and values, both past and present. (pp. 534–35)

The principal must have a working knowledge of curriculum areas, but it is more important that the principal facilitate the development of curriculum and review of current trends and practices by teachers. The principal as curriculum leader must facilitate the development of the teachers' knowledge of the new curriculum frameworks, place attention on the curriculum development process, and provide professional development to bring about needed curriculum changes. The principal keeps the clarity of focus to help develop a school curriculum that supports the learning community's vision for student learning.

REFLECTIONS: AS A NEW PRINCIPAL, HOW WOULD YOU PURSUE

CURRICULUM DEVELOPMENT AT YOUR SCHOOL? WRITE DOWN

YOUR THOUGHTS.

INSTRUCTIONAL PRACTICES

A learning community must have instructional practices that focus on creating the optimum experience for each student to learn. Instructional practices are the means by which the school carries out the approved curriculum. The principal must be knowledgeable in current instructional practices that complement the new curriculum. Research on effective teaching and effective schools in the 1970s and 1980s identified which teaching processes and school characteristics produced higher-than-average levels of student learning and thus produced effective schools. The findings confirmed that strategies of classroom management and teaching practices, as well as school organization variables, were linked to higher student learning (Cohen 1983).

The findings from the effective teaching research (Brophy 1992; Everston and Harris 1992) related to classroom management show that the more effective teachers:

- Maximized the time available for instruction.
- Maintained a smooth pace during lessons by being well prepared.
- Used transition activities that were organized, brief, and smooth.
- Taught students at the beginning of the year the rules governing classroom conduct, classroom procedures, and how materials would be used.

Also from the effective teaching research (Brophy 1992; Everston and Harris 1992), the findings related to classroom teaching processes reveal that the more effective teachers:

- Viewed teaching academic content as their primary task.
- Had a teaching day that was well planned and organized.
- Emphasized student mastery of curriculum and allocated most of their classroom time to active instruction.
- Engaged in active teaching, which entailed structuring the presentation of content, using advance organizers, summarizing key points, and reviewing main ideas.
- Presented information through interactive lessons, provided feedback through sequential questioning, and prepared students for seatwork, during which the students experienced success on eighty to ninety percent of academic tasks.
- Provided numerous opportunities for instruction and focused attention and praise on genuine student achievement and mastery.

The effective school's research goes hand in hand with the effective teaching practices and points to these critical elements (Edmonds 1979; Good and Brophy 1986):

- Strong instructional leadership, usually provided by the principal.
- Consensus on school goals that had an academic focus.
- Realistic but high expectations for student learning on the part of teachers as well as students.
- Emphasis on active instruction in the curriculum.
- A system of monitoring progress toward academic goals.
- Ongoing staff development.
- An orderly and secure environment with strong and consistently enforced student discipline program.

These research findings on effective schools and effective teaching showed that schools organized and managed with these key elements made a positive difference in student achievement. Berliner (1990) and Brophy (1992) state that these findings moved far beyond the testimonials and anecdotal findings of the past and began to provide a broader knowledge base for making educational practice more professional.

Although this research provided increased understanding about how schools make a difference, it did not address the more complex issues of how students learn to be thoughtful users and constructors of knowledge. Since then, cognitive science researchers have begun to study how to teach for understanding through the use of critical thinking and problem solving in the core content areas, providing an important basis for developing a student's cognitive abilities. The emphasis on instructional practices in the 1990s has focused on teaching students how to engage in high-level learning processes—to think, solve problems, communicate clearly, work in collegial groups, and apply these cognitive skills to everyday problems.

Lewis (1990, 534–35) identifies the following key instructional practices that have arisen from the cognitive development research about how to enhance students' cognitive capabilities:

- Active, constructivist student learning.
- Engaging students in issues, problems, and dilemmas in a real-life, practical context.
- Reading, listening, discussing, and writing across different content areas as ways to learn basic skills, facts, and knowledge as well as to solve problems.
- Reading, listening, discussing, and writing about great books in literature, history, mathematics, and science.
- Cooperative learning.

These emerging findings from cognitive research are transforming knowledge about how students learn and the roles that curriculum, teaching, and assessment play in the process of creating successful schools.

In the 1990s educators are looking at the findings of cognitive scientists and their research on learning, including the need for teaching higher-order thinking skills to all students, not just the brighter ones (Resnick 1987). The changing economy and the demand in the business world for thinking individuals have reinforced the research of the cognitive scientists to understand learning and thinking. Reviews of cognitive science research found the following points of new understanding about intelligence (Bransford, Goldman, and Vye 1991):

- Intelligence is multidimensional (Gardner 1983, 1991).
- Intelligence can be performed in everyday settings, and intelligence in daily settings (one's job) is at least as important as academic intelligence.
- Intelligence is not fixed at birth but can be developed, enhanced, and expanded over time.

According to Bransford, Goldman, and Vye (1991), these new views on intelligence have important implications for schools, principals, and teachers:

- Schools should switch from relying heavily on academic tasks to using everyday tasks (i.e., writing to a particular audience, reading to learn concepts and information needed to solve problems, analyzing data from experiments in everyday settings).

■ The new understandings of intelligence expand teachers' and parents' notions of what it means to be smart.

■ The notion of intelligence as developmental and how to develop everybody's intelligence over time not simply to identify and take as fixed intelligence difference.

Recent research on advanced cognitive knowledge and thinking identifies eight key points about learning that are significant for principals and teachers to bear in mind as they hone their instructional practices (Elmore 1991; Resnick 1987; Resnick and Klopfer 1989):

■ Learning is constructivist. Learners must create their own knowledge; it cannot be taught by teachers.

■ Learning develops best when individuals grapple with everyday, practical problems that require the active management of different types of knowledge, constructs, and processes.

■ Learning begins at very early ages (in babies, children in preschool, and elementary school students); young children can construct knowledge.

■ Learning does not occur alone but through social interaction.

■ Thinking is not an advanced skill but a part of all learning tasks.

■ Learning is not content-free but occurs in the context of specific bodies of knowledge.

■ As they approach learning tasks, individuals bring very different understanding, knowledge, and preconceptions, which teachers must recognize, understand, and use to develop the students' cognitive capabilities successfully.

■ Learning and thinking are not courses to be added to a curriculum, but an orientation to be infused throughout the day and a disposition to develop in the classroom, school, office, and at home.

By understanding trends in instructional practices, the principal can help the school learning community learn, practice, and implement the best instructional strategies to meet the diverse learning needs of students and deliver the designed curriculum. By keeping informed on the latest research and systematically reviewing the ongoing teaching and learning within the school, the learning community can work toward providing the best learning environment for each student.

Instructional practices are crucial to whether learning takes place and the curriculum is implemented, and the principal plays a key facilitative role in raising teachers' awareness and using the best instructional strategies to meet the needs of the school.

REFLECTIONS: AS A PRINCIPAL, WHAT ARE THE INSTRUCTIONAL
PRACTICES YOU WOULD HELP PROMOTE FOR INCREASED STU-
DENT ACHIEVEMENT? HOW WOULD YOU DEAL WITH INSTRUC-
TIONAL PRACTICE ISSUES? WRITE DOWN YOUR THOUGHTS.

ASSESSMENT

The principal as facilitator must establish accountability for the progress of students, the curriculum, and instructional practices through ongoing assessment practices within the learning community. The role of assessment has seen unprecedented change in the last decade with the movement toward "authentic" or performance-based assessment (Stiggins 1994; Wiggins 1993). There is a trend away from standardized, or norm-referenced, testing to performance-based testing that is embedded in the curriculum over the course of the school year and provides information about not only what students know but also what they can do (Office of Technology Assessment 1992; Wiggins 1993). Many educators see this change as reinventing the technology for assessment with new approaches that move "beyond the bubble" of multiple-choice, paper-and-pencil tests (Wiggins 1993; Resnick 1991).

In reviewing assessment practices, Resnick (1991) found that standardized tests reflect an outmoded form of learning in that they fail to evaluate student performance according to new curriculum standards, reflect recent developments in understanding how students acquire knowledge, or produce equitable results among students regardless of ethnicity and gender. Standardized tests are at odds with the new research on learning. Norm-referenced test imply a "bell curve" of performance that places some students at the high end, many in the middle, and some at the low end; this is clearly inconsistent with the national goal of raising all students to higher levels of achievement (Resnick and Resnick 1992; Wiggins 1993). Norm-referenced tests suggest that knowledge can exist without any context; learning is focused on facts and data, not on concepts and connections;

a problem has only one solution, rather than multiple steps; learning is individual, not social; and knowledge and learning are abstract and academic, rather than connected to the real world. Thus, the prevailing approach to accountability through standardized tests is at odds with new curriculum and instructional practices that encourage students to be engaged in learning.

As a principal works with the learning community to improve student performance, developing the right approach to assessing students is critical. It is important that the principal understands assessment and avoids giving mixed messages about the learning goals of the school—one from the curriculum taught and another from the method of assessing the student (Stiggins 1994).

The principal can help guide and support the restructuring of assessment so that it evaluates the curriculum that is taught and the programs that the school offers. Currently, standardized testing is being replaced with performance-based assessment, which uses scoring rubrics that show all students performing at certain levels of behavior along with expectations for improved performance. Assessments must reinforce the chosen curriculum and philosophy of learning based on the beliefs that all students can attain high levels of thinking expertise in the core content areas and that all students will learn over time (National Commission on Time and Learning 1994). New forms of accountability assume that, even though some students might need more time or more explicit instruction than others, all students can achieve considerable expertise in thinking and problem-solving in the content areas.

Thus, performance-based assessment is the emerging alternative to norm-referenced testing (Stiggins 1994). This method determines student knowledge by assessing student performance in using knowledge to solve a problem, write a persuasive essay, or solve a multiple-step mathematics problem. Performance-based assessment makes use of open-ended questions, long-term projects, and portfolios and requires students to construct responses using agreed-upon criteria (Stiggins 1994; Wiggins 1993). In performance-based assessment, there may be multiple correct answers for a question or problem. This type of assessment requires students to assimilate concepts and facts for the purpose of performing a task, may ask students to justify and explain their answers rather than just provide an answer, and may include group interaction. The principle that guides performance-based assessment is that it must reflect the type of learning and knowledge embedded in the curriculum taught. Baker, O'Neil, and Linn (1993) state that performance-based assessments should:

- Use open-ended tasks.
- Focus on higher order or complex skills.
- Employ problem-focused and context-sensitive strategies.

■ Be performance-based and provide significant student time to complete.

■ Consist of both individual and group activities.

■ Involve a considerable degree of student choice. (p. 1210)

In evaluating student results, performance-based assessment must reflect explicit standards of rating and judgment that the student understands as well as the teacher. The scoring is done by rubrics that reflect the expertise level of the student's performance, such as basic, proficient, advanced or novice, apprentice, proficient, and distinguished levels. Performanced-based assessment assumes implicitly that with enough appropriate instruction, all students can achieve at the basic level and nearly all at the proficient level (Stiggins 1994; Wiggins 1993). A curriculum-embedded assessment allows for more frequent gathering of performance tasks for each student throughout the school year, thus enhancing the reliability of the combined results and providing immediate feedback to the teacher on the success of instructional practices (Guskey 1994).

A school learning community needs to be accountable for student learning and assessment practices. The principal must lead and facilitate discussion about assessment practices so that the school focuses on accountability for student learning (Stiggins 1994; Wiggins 1993). The principal and teachers must collaborate to develop, monitor, and review assessment practices in light of the school's curriculum and instructional strategies.

REFLECTIONS: AS A PRINCIPAL WORKING WITH A LEARNING COMMUNITY, WHAT ARE THE ASSESSMENT PRACTICES THAT YOU WOULD EXPECT TO SEE IMPLEMENTED THAT REFLECT EXEMPLARY PRACTICE? HOW DO THE CURRENT ASSESSMENT PRACTICES IN THE SCHOOL REFLECT THE CURRICULUM AND INSTRUCTION PROGRAM? WRITE DOWN YOUR THOUGHTS.

SUMMARY

A school learning community must hold curriculum, instruction, and assessment central to its work if it expects to make a difference for student learning. The principal's role has evolved from manager to instructional leader to facilitator-leader of the school learning community. Through the collaborative work of the principal and teachers, curriculum development and instructional and assessment practices continually change to conform to the needs of all students. Curriculum, instruction, and assessment are the heart of the school learning community. The role of the principal is to facilitate and keep the school focused on excellent curriculum, instruction, and assessment to meet students' learning needs and improve achievement.

REFLECTIVE ACTIVITIES

1. Curriculum, Instruction, and Assessment Issues

What are the current curriculum, instruction, and assessment issues at your school? Pick one of the curriculum, instruction, or assessment issues presented in this chapter and analyze the key questions that arise for the school learning community (teachers, students, principal, parents, and other community members) regarding this issue. How do these key questions relate to what you have learned about the role of the principal in curriculum, instruction, or assessment?

2. Interview a Principal About Curriculum, Instruction, and Assessment

Interview a principal about the role of a principal in developing curriculum, instruction, and assessment. What insights have you gained after reflecting on the interview? How would you define the role of the principal in relation to curriculum, instruction, and assessment?

3. Interview a Superintendent About the Principal's Role in Curriculum, Instruction, and Assessment

Interview a superintendent about perceptions of the principal's role in curriculum, instruction, and assessment. What insights have you gained from the superintendent's perceptions? How does this help you define the role of the principal in relation to curriculum, instruction, and assessment?

SUGGESTED READINGS

Goldring, Ellen B., and Sharon F. Rallis. 1993. *Principals of Dynamic Schools*. Newbury Park, CA: Corwin Press.

Murphy, Joseph, and Phillip Hallinger. 1993. *Restructuring Schooling: Learning from Ongoing Efforts*. Newbury Park, CA: Corwin Press.

Odden, Allan R. 1995. *Educational Leadership for America's Schools*. New York: McGraw-Hill.

Wiggins, Grant. 1993. *Assessing Student Performance*. San Francisco: Jossey-Bass.

REFERENCES

Baker, Eva L., Harold F. O'Neil, and Robert L. Linn. 1993. Policy and Validity Prospects for Performance-Based Assessment. *American Psychologist* 48(12): 1210–1218.

Beck, Lynn G., and Joseph Murphy. 1993. *Understanding the Principal*. New York: Teachers College Press.

Berliner, David. 1990. If the Metaphor Fits, Why Not Wear It? The Teacher as Executive. *Theory into Practice* 24(20): 85–93.

Bransford, John, Susan Goldman, and Nancy Vye. 1991. Making a Difference in People's Abilities to Think: Reflections on a Decade of Work and Some Hopes for the Future. In *Directions of Development: Influence on Children's Thinking*, edited by Lynn Okagaki and Robert J. Sternberg, 147–180. Hillsdale, NJ: Erlbaum.

Brophy, Jere. 1992. Probing the Subtleties of Subject Matter Teaching. *Educational Leadership* 49(7): 4–8.

Cohen, Michael. 1983. Instruction, Management, and Organizational Issues in Effective Schools. In *School Finance and School Improvement: Linkages for the 1980s*, edited by Allan Odden and L. Dean Webb. Cambridge, MA: Ballinger.

Cordeiro, Paula. 1994. The Principal's Role in Curricular Leadership and Program Development. Chap. 7 in *The Principal as Leader*, edited by Larry W. Hughes, 161–183. Upper Saddle River, NJ: Merrill/Prentice Hall.

Edmonds, Ronald. 1979. Effective Schools for the Urban Poor. *Educational Leadership* 37(1): 15–24.

Elmore, Richard F. 1991. Teaching, Learning, and Organization: School Restructuring and the Recurring Dilemmas of Reform. Address presented to the annual meeting of the American Education Research Association, Chicago, 1991.

Everston, Carolyn M., and Arlene H. Harris. 1992. What We Know About Managing Classrooms. *Educational Leadership* 49(7): 74–78.

Gardner, Howard. 1983. *Frames of Mind*. New York: Basic Books.

Gardner, Howard. 1991. *The Unschooled Mind: How Children Think and How Schools Should Teach*. New York: Basic Books.

Goldring, Ellen B., and Sharon F. Rallis. 1993. *Principals of Dynamic Schools*. Newbury Park, CA: Corwin Press.

Good, Thomas, and Jere Brophy. 1986. School Effects. In *Handbook of Research on Teaching*, edited by Merlin Wittrock, 570–602. New York: Macmillan.

Greenfield, William. 1987. *Instructional Leadership: Concepts, Issues, and Controversies*. Boston: Allyn and Bacon.

Guskey, Thomas. 1994. *High-Stakes Performance Assessment*. Thousand Oaks, CA: Corwin Press.

Leithwood, Kenneth A. 1992. The Move Toward Transformational Leadership. *Educational Leadership* 49(5): 8–12.

Lewis, Anne C. 1990. Getting Unstuck: Curriculum As a Tool of Reform. *Phi Delta Kappan* (7): 534–35.

Murphy, Joseph. 1990. Principal Instructional Leadership. In *Advances In Educational Administration, Vol. I, Part B: Changing Perspectives on the School*, edited by Paul Thurston and Linda Lotto, 163–200. Greenwich, CT: JAI Press.

Murphy, Joseph. 1994. Transformational Change and the Evolving Role of the Principal: Early Empirical Evidence. In *Reshaping the Principalship: Insights from Transformational Change Efforts*, edited by Joseph Murphy and Karen Seashore Louis. Newbury Park, CA: Corwin Press.

Murphy, Joseph, and Phillip Hallinger. 1993. *Restructuring Schooling: Learning from Ongoing Efforts*. Newbury Park, CA: Corwin Press.

National Commission on Time and Learning. 1994. *Prisoners of Time*. Washington, DC: U.S. Department of Education.

Odden, Allan R. 1995. *Educational Leadership for America's Schools*. New York: McGraw-Hill.

Office of Technology Assessment. 1992. *Testing in American Schools: Asking the Right Questions*, OTA-SET-519. Washington, DC: U.S. Government Printing Office.

Prager, Karen. 1993. Collegial Process versus Curricular Focus: Dilemma for Principal Leadership. *Brief 5*. Madison, WI: University of Wisconsin, Wisconsin Center for Educational Research, Center on Organization and Restructuring of Schools.

Resnick, Lauren. 1987. *Education and Learning to Think*. Washington, DC: National Academy of Education.

Resnick, Lauren. 1991. Testimony before the Senate Committee on Labor and Human Resources, Subcommittee on Education, Arts, and the Humanities, March 7, 1991.

Resnick, Lauren, and Leopold E. Klopfer, eds. 1989. *Toward the Thinking Curriculum: Current Cognitive Research*. Washington, DC: Association for Supervision and Curriculum Development.

Resnick, Lauren, and Daniel P. Resnick. 1992. Assessing the Thinking Curriculum: New Tools for Educational Reform. In *Changing Assessments: Alternative Views of Aptitude, Achievement, and Instruction*, edited by Bernard R. Gifford and Mary Catherine O'Connor, 37–75. Boston, MA: Kluwer Academic.

Stiggins, Richard J. 1994. *Student-Centered Classroom Assessment*. Upper Saddle River, NJ: Merrill/Prentice Hall.

Wiggins, Grant. 1993. *Assessing Student Performance*. San Francisco: Jossey-Bass.

CHAPTER 8

PROFESSIONAL DEVELOPMENT

PROBLEM SCENARIO

You have just been appointed principal of a school—its third in just five years. You are determined to work with the teachers and district to build a learning community that continuously strives to improve learning for its students. How does professional development figure into your plans? What professional development will engender improved practice? Remember, practically the entire staff is suspicious of yet another principal coming in with a new agenda.

THE IMPORTANCE OF PROFESSIONAL DEVELOPMENT

Schools have long neglected the systematic professional development of teachers, staff, and administrators. More often than not, efforts to improve schools have dealt with professional development on a hit-or-miss basis. One-day workshops come and go, with virtually no impact on the school. It is little wonder that teachers are cool when presented with new ideas and programs touching on professional development without follow-up or planning. Recognizing the link between professional development and educational improvement provides the fundamental source of ongoing renewal and reflection on practice for schools (Sparks and Hirsh 1997). The sustained development of the professionals is the heart of a continually growing learning community. It is through the constant pursuit of knowledge and reflection on the application of that knowledge that a school becomes a learning community. The principal's role in promoting, facilitating, and participating in professional development is integral to developing a school culture where educators are continual learners.

The current demographic, social, and political context of schooling demands teachers who are deeply knowledgeable about children, families, culture, and community relationships, as well as about curriculum and pedagogical practices. Educators working in this climate face complex, unprecedented challenges. They must address the needs of students of differing ethnic backgrounds with diverse economic and social obstacles and prepare them for life in a society that demands sophisticated knowledge and skills.

In this dynamic and demanding setting, educators can no longer settle for the old type of teacher: an isolated practitioner, alone in a classroom. Educators themselves—including principals, teachers, and staff—must continually acquire and share new knowledge, skills, resources, and ways of doing their jobs. As with most other types of professionals, educators must be lifelong learners. Striving to become continually engaged in the process of change and reinvention to meet the changing needs of students should be the central work of a school learning community, according to Senge (O'Neil 1995). How does this happen, and what does a principal who wants to build a learning community need to know about professional development? This chapter deals with professional development as a key ingredient for developing and sustaining a learning community.

Professional development for educators is a critical component of educational reform meant to help schools meet the challenges of the twenty-first century. Over the past decade, there have been great demands and initiatives for school reform, but there remains a paucity of methods for equipping educators with the skills and other means they need to effect school reform. If professional development programs are to improve learning for teachers, and consequently for students, they must be effectively designed and implemented. For that to happen, such programs must have solid grounding in what research and experience tells us is effective.

Over the last decade, the educational reform movement in the United States has conducted research that clarifies the essentials of "best practice" in professional development for sustaining educational change (USSER Professional Development Task Force 1997). Until schools base professional development on "best practice" and provide learning and growth opportunities, teachers, staff, and administrators will not meet the demands of educational reform, nor will they develop into learning communities. Professional development engenders renewal, reflection, and dialogue among education professionals about schooling. It allows a learning community to expand its ability to achieve desired goals, nurture new and expansive patterns of thinking and teaching methods, set free its members' collective aspirations, and become a place where people learn how to learn together (Senge 1990).

What are the essentials of "best practice" in professional development that our schools can use to initiate and sustain systemic educational change and help the school learning community grow? Educators must consider their daily interactions with students and with one another as they look at what really works according to the research on "best practice" to develop a solid foundation for their efforts at in-service training, workshops, staff-sharing time, and other means of professional development. There is a fundamental mismatch between the demands of educational reform and the professional development opportunities afforded teachers and administrators, the very people charged with bringing about sustained improvement in education for students and educators (Hargreaves 1997).

Given what is known about the research on "best practice" in professional development, why do educators continue to approach professional development in outmoded, ineffective ways that yield only short-term improvement? The principal and others in the learning community must discover new ways—consistent with research on best practice—to promote professional development, if they are to improve their school.

EXPLORING A PROFESSIONAL DEVELOPMENT MODEL FOR SUSTAINED CHANGE

A learning community must establish a culture for continuous professional development. The Essentials of Best Practice in Professional Development for Sustained Change Model (see Figure 8.1) presents a means of engaging a learning community in systematic professional development. The model provides a synthesis of the growing body of research, not only in professional development, but also in adult learning theory, shared leadership, effective schools, and the change process (Fullan 1993; Lieberman and Miller 1992; Lieberman 1995a; Darling-Hammond and McLaughlin 1995; Hargreaves 1997; Sparks and Hirsh 1997). It is not so much a model as an example for studying profes-

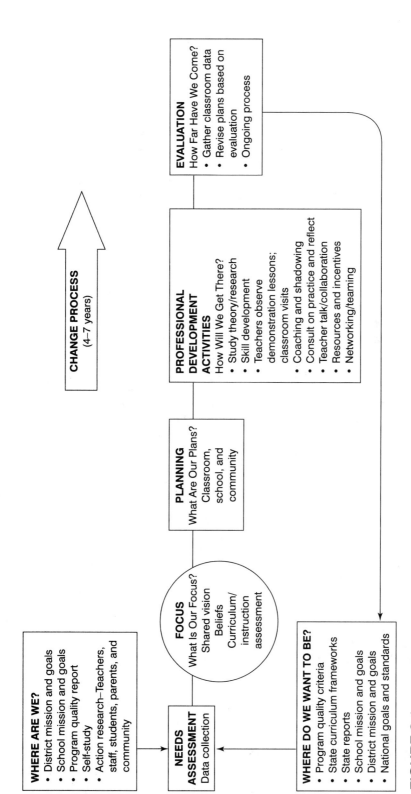

FIGURE 8.1
Essentials of Best Practice

sional development. A learning community can use this model to design and review their professional development efforts based on "best practices." District administrators, principals, and teachers must have tools to analyze professional development practices before they will stop using old methods of professional development that do not work. The model hopefully will serve as the framework for a learning community to develop a culture of professional development.

As a learning community begins to look at its educational reform efforts, its members should establish an overview of the professional development process. The model in Figure 8.1 (Speck 1996) provides such an overview, looking at educational change that will take four to seven years of dedicated efforts. The key elements of the process are: conducting a needs assessment, developing a focus or shared vision, planning, engaging in professional development activities, and preparing an evaluation plan with an ongoing revision process. To elaborate on this model, members of the learning community may study and answer the key focus areas and specific questions in the Planning Professional Development (see Figure 8.2) guide as they develop professional development plans and activities. These focus areas and questions help a learning community answer the key issues in assessing needs, providing focus, planning to meet the needs, originating effective professional development activities, and evaluating progress and revising plans to better meet the needs of the learning community.

Using a professional development model gives a learning community a broad look at what must happen for sustained change within the school. Too often, educators simply jump on the latest bandwagon of educational innovations, which can include one-day workshops by outside experts, short presentations to the faculty, periodic school visitations, and other quick awareness sessions that do not have the essential elements of what we know are "best practice" in professional development. It is little wonder, then, that educators cannot significantly improve their schools. Professional development is not a quick fix, but a long-term commitment to continual learning, reflecting on practice, and changing practices in a systematic way that reinforces the learning community's drive to improve student success.

Sparks and Hirsh (1997) substantiate the problem that has existed for schools experiencing change and their ill-fated attempts at professional development:

> Schools have long been criticized for their fragmented approach to change. Too often, critics charge, school improvement has been based on fad rather than a clear vision of the school system's future. This, in turn, has led to one-shot staff [professional] development workshops of the "dog-and-pony-show" variety, with little consideration of how the program will continue or how this partic-

Focus Areas and Questions

Needs Assessment

- Where are we?
  - District mission and goals
  - School mission and goals
  - Program quality report
  - Self-study report
  - Action research—teachers
  - Staff, students, parents, and other community members
- Where do we want to be?
  - Program quality criteria
  - State curriculum frameworks
  - State and national reports
  - School mission and goals
  - District mission and goals
  - National goals and standards
- What data do we need?
- What does our needs assessment reveal?

Focus

- What is our clear focus?
- What are our beliefs?
- What is our shared vision?
- How does our focus relate to curriculum, instruction, and assessment?

Planning

- What are our plans in the classroom, school, district, and community?

Professional Development Activities

- How will we get there?
- What are the professional development activities, and do they match "best practices"?
  - Study theory and research
  - Develop skills
  - Observe demonstration lessons; make classroom visits
  - Practice lessons
  - Coach and shadow
  - Consult and reflect on practice
  - Talk and collaborate with other teachers
  - Make resources and incentives available
  - Create networking and teaming

Evaluation

- How far have we come?
- What data do we have to assess the effectiveness of our plan and professional development activities?
- How do we revise our plans and professional development activities based on ongoing evaluation?

FIGURE 8.2

Planning Professional Development

ular event fits in with earlier efforts. At its worst, this form of staff [professional] development asks teachers and administrators to implement poorly understood innovation with little support. Before they are able to master the new technique or skill, the school has moved on to other topics.[1]

THE COMPONENTS OF BEST PRACTICE IN PROFESSIONAL DEVELOPMENT

The rest of this chapter addresses the essential components of best practice in professional development, as derived from recent research. Principals, teachers, and other members of the learning community should strive to understand and practice these components with the goal of generating and sustaining change:

- Research-based focus on increased student learning
- School-based, diversified, integrated, and ongoing lifelong process
- Opportunities and time for learning in daily practice (job-embedded)
- Risk-taking, respect, responsibility, and recognition
- Providing resources
- Planning and implementation using adult learning theory
- Assessing progress

RESEARCH-BASED FOCUS ON INCREASED STUDENT LEARNING

Educators must never forget that the objective of professional development is to increase student learning. Professional development programs should be based on research, including studies from sources outside the schools as well as "action research," in which educators test the impact of theories and methods on their own students' success. When selecting a professional development program, teachers and principals

---

[1] From *A New Vision for Staff Development* by Dennis Sparks and Stephanie Hirsh, p. 24. Alexandria, Va: Association for Supervision and Curriculum Development. Copyright © 1997 by ASCD. Reprinted by permission. All rights reserved.

should examine the available research to determine whether that program improved student learning and, if so, whether their own students are similar to the research population. Many powerful teaching strategies have been shown to stimulate particular kinds of learning and improve learning in certain student populations. But, because students of differing backgrounds respond differently, a school must select educational programs carefully, avoiding the "one size fits all" pitfall.

Rather than basing professional development solely on educators' perceptions of their own needs—for example, to learn about classroom management—schools should begin professional development planning by determining what students need to know, then work backward to pinpoint the knowledge, skills, and attitudes educators must have. This emphasis on student needs does not negate teachers' perceptions of their needs; instead, it provides a larger context for those needs. Educators must judge professional development activities on how they affect student learning, not solely by the participants' satisfaction. Professional development must improve student learning (Caldwell 1989; Lieberman 1995b; Darling-Hammond and McLaughlin 1995; Sparks and Hirsh 1997).

SCHOOL-BASED, DIVERSIFIED, AND INTEGRATED LIFELONG PROCESS

The school is the largest unit of change, and so a district improves school by school. Thus, the school must be the primary focus of and impetus for professional learning and improved practice. Professional development programs at the district level should be aligned with the needs of specific schools; they should support the work of schools rather than determine schools' plans. District efforts should be aimed at helping schools meet their goals for improvement. The district can provide technical assistance and support schools' efforts toward professional development (Fullan 1993; Lieberman 1995a; Darling-Hammond and McLaughlin 1995; Sparks and Hirsh 1997).

The incremental nature of professional development means it will take four to seven years to make significant changes in educational practices. Such goals as instilling values of improvement and continuous learning in a school's culture require long-range strategies bolstered by short-range planning, not the one-shot infusion typified by a daylong seminar or workshop. Teachers should be able to choose from a range of learning options and should have multiple opportunities to meet their individual needs as well as those of the school. Thus, effective professional development is a diverse and ongoing process, a lifelong endeavor to improve professionally, with the end being improved education of students (Caldwell 1989; Joyce and Showers 1995; Darling-Hammond and McLaughlin 1995; Sparks and Hirsh 1997).

All educators should be deeply engaged in learning throughout their careers. As Rubin (1971) stated, the minute that educators end their education, they start down the road to incompetence. Given the inherent intellectual challenges of their jobs, teachers, principals, and staff members must have opportunities to stimulate each other's growth by engaging in intellectual conversations about teaching and learning. At the same time, they need formal structures such as journal writing, team teaching, collaboratives, networking, and subject-matter projects that supply them with reasons to reflect on their craft, both individually and collectively, and engage in the larger communities of practice outside the school. These intellectual activities can help teachers build competency, optimism, connections, and inner resources to sustain them through the rigors of the classroom. The learning community must foster a culture of continual learning and reflection on the part of each learning community member. The principal must daily stimulate and sustain professional development through meaningful conversations and other forms of interaction with others at the school. Figure 8.3 identifies some professional development opportunities a principal can afford a school in a systemic way to help sustain change or implement new programs within a learning community (Caldwell 1989; Darling-Hammond and McLaughlin 1995; Lieberman 1995b).

REFLECTIONS: AS A PRINCIPAL, HOW WOULD YOU WORK WITH

YOUR LEARNING COMMUNITY TO PROVIDE PROFESSIONAL

DEVELOPMENT OPPORTUNITIES? WRITE DOWN YOUR THOUGHTS.

OPPORTUNITIES AND TIME FOR LEARNING IN DAILY PRACTICE

Teachers and principals need time to discuss, try out, reflect on, and hone new practices, as well as to learn more about curriculum, pedagogy, assessment, and the needs of students. Teachers and principals must be involved in learning about, developing, and using new ideas. This collaborative work might involve taking on new roles, for example, teacher-leader, peer coach, or teacher-researcher; participating in new structures, such as problem-solving groups, decision-making teams, school-based research teams, or peer review; and working on new tasks, which might include proposal writing, learning about assessment, developing standards, or analyzing or writing case studies

FIGURE 8.3

Professional Development Opportunities That Learning Communities Should Encourage

From "Best Practice in Professional Development for Sustained Educational Change," by Marsha Speck, 1996, *ERS Spectrum-Journal of School Research and Information,* 4(2) pp. 33–41.

- Studying theory and research of practice
- Developing skills and knowledge of practice
- Demonstrating and observing practice in workshops and classrooms
- Receiving feedback on practice
- Providing resources for practice
- Shadowing an expert practitioner
- Coaching by an expert or peer coach
- Consulting and reflecting on practice
- Collaborating on practice
- Creating networking and teaming for practice

of practice. These in-school professional development activities require support for both individual and collective learning. The principal needs to ensure that teachers have opportunities to engage in such professional development activities. Methods of doing so include altering work schedules, helping schedule activities, and monitoring these professional development opportunities. By encouraging professional growth and collegial interaction, the principal exemplifies the vision of a learning community. The principal serves as an advocate for teachers who are exploring and implementing new practices and collaborative efforts of gaining knowledge (Little 1993; Fullan 1993; Darling-Hammond and McLaughlin 1995; Sagor 1992; Wiggins 1993).

After participating in professional development programs, the most well-intentioned teachers and principals tend to fall back into old habits when they return to school. It takes considerable practice for teachers and principals to become comfortable with new knowledge and techniques and incorporate them in their professional beliefs and work. To transfer a new mind-set into daily practice, an educator must get follow-up assistance, coaching, mentoring, and other forms of helpful feedback and reinforcement in employing new skills and behaviors. Recent research indicates there is very little internalization, application, or transfer of skills into the classroom or workplace unless there are demonstrations, practice, feedback opportunities, ongoing coaching and periodic review that follow initial learning opportunities. Follow-up on professional development activities provides the support and coaching that help a person master new skills, develop lessons, and instructional practices essential to changes in curriculum and instruction (Joyce and Showers 1995; Little 1993; Lieberman 1995a).

Professional development can mean learning from colleagues and personal experience rather than from an outside expert, as in the traditional model of learning. Teachers see the most improvement in their practices when they take an active role in articulating problems, exploring solutions, and applying new techniques. They should be able to share what they have learned in daily exchanges and collaborations with fellow teachers. In this way, professional development focuses on these "communities of practice" within a school, rather than simply on teachers as individuals. The "action research" method is a way for teachers to explore their practices and develop solutions (Sagor 1992). A learning community culture nurtures the quest for knowledge and new teaching practices that will improve student achievement (Lieberman 1995b; Darling-Hammond, Ancess, and Falk 1995; Joyce and Showers 1995).

RISK-TAKING, RESPECT, RESPONSIBILITY, AND RECOGNITION

Successful professional development programs address the web of values, norms, and beliefs that shape a learning community. The principal must be aware of these values and norms and find ways to establish a school culture that supports risk-taking, respects teachers as professionals, and encourages intellectual curiosity and professional growth. If a school's culture is characterized by a belief that teachers are powerless and ineffectual, teachers there are unlikely to contribute to efforts at improvement. When teachers feel isolated in their classrooms, their chances for collaboration or collegiality are almost nil. A principal can help avert this by providing opportunities for teachers to work together. This demands the principal's daily attention, but the reward can be a learning community that sees professional growth in individuals members and in the collective whole (Lieberman 1995a; Lieberman and Miller 1992; Darling-Hammond, Ancess, and Falk 1995; Joyce and Showers 1995).

Teachers need to make a commitment and take responsibility to implement new programs and practice—individually and collectively—before they will want to participate in professional development. Those who will be affected by changes should have a voice in the process and be held responsible for the outcome. Thus, teachers need to participate in planning and making decisions about improvements and systemic changes. It is also important that teachers have the power to initiate changes aimed at meeting the needs of students. These include decisions on such matters as schedules, curriculum, personnel, space, and materials. Schools should be organized around small, cohesive units, such as teaching teams or clusters, houses, or advisory groups, allowing for ongoing collaboration among adults and students and offering teachers shared access to students and shared responsibilities for designing their work. For collaborative efforts to work well, relationships within the school must allow for communication. Working together on common projects and problems, teachers and principals can establish the constructive culture of a learning community (Deal and Kennedy 1982; Sizer 1996; Saphier and King 1985; Darling-Hammond and McLaughlin 1995).

Teachers need and deserve recognition for their efforts to implement new professional practices, just as principals do. Unfortunately, current supervisory practices often foster mediocrity, discourage innovation, and destroy any motivation or responsibility to make changes. Instead, a principal must find ways to structure supervision and evaluation to recognize and reward teachers who demonstrate intellectual curiosity, are committed to professional growth, and apply their new knowledge and skills to improving education. A principal's supervisory policies should reflect the important link between professional development and improvements in curriculum and instruction. As leader of the learning community, the principal must ensure that teachers know about other teachers' efforts to improve education and ensure that those efforts are rewarded as well as that teachers be held accountable for results (Darling-Hammond, Ancess, and Falk 1995; Darling-Hammond and McLaughlin 1995; Fullan 1993; Glickman 1993; Lieberman 1995a; Hargreaves 1997).

PROVIDING RESOURCES

School districts have primary responsibility for providing the resources—time, money, personnel, and materials—that a school needs to implement programs and instructional practices through professional development activities. But schools must join in the search for money to pay for these activities. The likelihood of making and sustaining such fundamental change is improbable unless schools get the money to pay for the ongoing educational efforts that encourage professional development and, thereby, school improvement. In part because the budget is seen as a measure of the district's priorities, if resources for professional development become inadequate, teachers are likely to become disillusioned with efforts to improve the school and thus revert to old ways of doing things. Providing resources for training, demonstration, practice, coaching, feedback, and collaboration is a key role for the principal in professional development because simple exposure to ideas is inadequate for the growth of a culture of professionalism. To ensure that learning is reinforced, a principal must review the budget and find ways to stretch allocations to pay for continued professional development (Little 1993; Fullan 1993; Hargreaves 1997; Darling-Hammond and McLaughlin 1995).

PLANNING AND IMPLEMENTATION USING ADULT LEARNING THEORY

If professional development programs are to be effective, their design and implementation should be based on adult learning theory, which includes the following principles drawn from Joyce and Showers (1995), the National Staff Development Council (1995), and Little (1993):

- Adults will commit to learning when they believe that the objectives are realistic and important for their personal and professional needs. They need to see that what they learn through professional development is relevant and applicable to their day-to-day activities and problems.

- Adults want to be the origin of their own learning and should thus have some control over the what, who, how, why, when, and where of their learning.

- Adult will resist activities that they see as an attack on their competence. Professional development must be structured to provide support from peers and reduce the fear of judgment.

- Adult learners need direct, concrete experiences for applying what they have learned.

- Adult learners do not automatically transfer learning into daily practice. Coaching and other kinds of follow-up support are needed so that the learning is sustained.

- Adults need to receive feedback on their efforts. Professional development activities must include opportunities for individuals to practice new skills and receive structured, helpful feedback.

- Adults need to participate in small-group activities during the learning process. By providing an opportunity to share, reflect, and generalize their learning and experiences, these small groups help adult learners move from simply understanding the new material to the level of application, analysis, synthesis, and evaluation.

- Adult learners come to the learning process with self-direction and a range of previous experiences, knowledge, interests, and competencies. This diversity must be accommodated in planning and implementing professional development.

- Adults enjoy novelty in their learning experiences.

ASSESSING PROGRESS

A learning community must have assessment policies and practices that will measure the effectiveness of professional development activities on reaching the school's goals. Too often, professional development activities simply roll along from inertia with little analysis on their effectiveness. Evaluating such programs should draw on multiple sources of information, gauging the reactions of participants, measuring the participants' progress in the classroom as evidenced by the use of new knowledge and skills, and determining the resulting impact on student achievement. The results of these evaluations should then affect further planning for professional development (Joyce and Showers 1995; National Staff Development Council 1995; Little 1993; Hargreaves 1997; Darling-Hammond and McLaughlin 1995).

SUMMARY

In this time of change and challenge for education, we can no longer abide the discrepancy between demands for educational reform and limited opportunities for educators to grow professionally. It is not enough simply to increase opportunities for growth, however. Professional development can contribute to sustained educational improvement, but only when based on solid, up-to-date research on best practices, effective planning and implementation, and clear objectives. This continued pursuit of knowledge and reflection on the application of that knowledge enables a school to become a learning community. The principal has an integral role in developing a culture of learning that puts a premium on educators who are continual learners, constantly growing as professionals.

REFLECTIVE ACTIVITIES

1. Analyzing Professional Development Activities in a School or District

Review the professional development activities of a school and/or district over the last three years, applying criteria from this chapter.

What does your analysis reveal about professional development activities and their effects on change in the school and/or district? What insights have you gained about planning and implementing professional development programs?

2. Interview a District's Professional Development Coordinator

Interview the professional development coordinator in your school district about the principles set forth in the model in Figure 8.1. What did you learn about professional development?

3. Design a Professional Development Plan

Based on the principles in the model in Figure 8.1 and other information you have gained about professional development from this chapter, draw up a three-year professional development plan for your school.

SUGGESTED READINGS

Darling-Hammond, Linda, and Milbrey McLaughlin. 1995. Policies That Support Professional Development in an Era of Reform. *Phi Delta Kappan* 76(8), 597–604.

Joyce, Bruce, and Beverly Showers. 1995. *Student Achievement Through Staff Development.* White Plains, NY: Longman.

Lieberman, Ann. 1995. Practices That Support Teacher Development: Transforming Conceptions of Professional Learning. *Phi Delta Kappan* 76(8), 591–596.

Sparks, Dennis, and Stephanie Hirsh. 1997. *A New Vision for Staff Development.* Alexandria, VA: Association for Supervision and Curriculum Development.

Speck, Marsha. 1996. Best Practice in Professional Development for Sustained Educational Change. *ERS Spectrum-Journal of School Research and Information* 4(2), 33–41.

REFERENCES

Caldwell, Sarah D., ed. 1989. *Staff Development: A Handbook of Effective Practice*. Oxford, OH: National Staff Development Council.

Darling-Hammond, Linda, and Milbrey McLaughlin. 1995. Policies That Support Professional Development in an Era of Reform. *Phi Delta Kappan* 76(8): 597–604.

Darling-Hammond, Linda, Jacqueline Ancess, and Beverly Falk. 1995. *Authentic Assessment in Action: Case Studies*. New York: Teachers College Press.

Deal, Terrence E., and Allan A. Kennedy. 1982. *Corporate Cultures: The Rites and Rituals of Corporate Life*. Reading, MA: Addison Wesley.

Fullan, Michael. 1993. *Change Forces: Probing the Depths of Educational Reform*. New York: Falmer Press.

Glickman, Carl D. 1993. *Renewing America's Schools: A Guide for School-Based Action*. San Francisco: Jossey-Bass.

Hargreaves, Andrew, ed. 1997. *Rethinking Educational Change with Heart and Mind*. Alexandria, VA: Association for Supervision and Curriculum Development.

Joyce, Bruce, and Beverly Showers. 1995. *Student Achievement Through Staff Development*. White Plains, NY: Longman.

Lieberman, Ann. 1995a. Practices That Support Teacher Development: Transforming Conceptions of Professional Learning. *Phi Delta Kappan* 76(8): 591–596.

Lieberman, Ann. 1995b. *The Work of Restructuring Schools: Building from the Ground Up*. New York: Teachers College Press.

Lieberman, Ann, and Lynne Miller. 1992. *Teachers: Their World and Their Work*. New York: Teachers College Press.

Little, Judith Warren. 1993. *Teachers' Professional Development in a Climate of Educational Reform*. New York: National Center for Restructuring Education, Schools, and Teaching, Teachers College, Columbia University.

National Staff Development Council. 1995. Standards for Staff Development. Oxford, OH: National Staff Development Council.

O'Neil, John. 1995. On Schools as Learning Organizations: A Conversation with Peter Senge. *Educational Leadership* 52(7), 20–23.

Rubin, Louis J. 1971. *In-Service Education of Teachers: Trends, Processes, and Prescriptions*. Boston: Allyn and Bacon.

Sagor, Richard. 1992. *How to Conduct Collaborative Action Research.* Alexandria, VA: Association for Supervision and Curriculum Development.

Saphier, Jon, and Matthew King. 1985. Good Seeds Grow in Strong Cultures. *Educational Leadership* 42(6): 67–74.

Senge, Peter. 1990. *The Fifth Discipline: The Art and Practice of the Learning Organization.* New York: Doubleday.

Sizer, Theodore. 1996. *Horace's Hope: What Works for the American High School.* Boston: Houghton Mifflin.

Sparks, Dennis, and Stephanie Hirsh. 1997. *A New Vision for Staff Development.* Alexandria, VA: Association for Supervision and Curriculum Development.

Speck, Marsha. 1996. Best Practice in Professional Development for Sustained Educational Change. *ERS Spectrum-Journal of School Research and Information* 4(2): 33–41.

University-School Support for Education Reform (USSER) Professional Development Task Force. 1997. *USSER Professional Development Task Force Report: Essential Questions and Practices in Professional Development.* San Francisco: USSER publication.

Wiggins, Grant. 1993. *Assessing Student Performance.* San Francisco: Jossey-Bass.

CHAPTER 9

BUDGET DEVELOPMENT

As principal, you are respon-
sible for the school's operation and management. What role
does the budget process play in your aims to engage the rest
of the learning community in improving general conditions and
learning? What crucial issues must you face when dealing with
the budget? How would you draw the rest of the learning community into developing the budget?

IMPORTANCE OF BUDGET DEVELOPMENT

If schools are to improve learning for the diverse student population
and educators, the budget and other resources that support instruction
must be addressed. Historically, school budgets have followed traditional allocation formulas set by a district office business department,
state and federal mandates, and union contracts. Typically school officials in general and school principals in particular see the budget
process as filling in the appropriate boxes so the ledger "adds up" at
the end of the year. This time-honored practice makes rethinking the

budget and the use of resources more difficult for a learning community. Likewise, specific requirements and constraints such as state and federal monitoring are major stumbling blocks to finding creative ways of using school resources. In fact, most federal mandates are underfunded, further straining schools' budgets. Therefore, it is important for a learning community to rethink and redo the budget, bringing it into alignment with the needs and values of the school. The learning community, led by the principal, must regard budget development as a means of fulfilling the school's vision.

Drake and Roe (1994) point out the importance of understanding and utilizing the budget development process as it relates to the role of the principal in improving the school:

> Too often the lack of money is blamed for the lack of innovative teaching-learning situations. It is true that more money can make a good program better by providing more alternatives to the users. Yet, many of the variations . . . do not require more money. They may merely demand the reordering of priorities. It is recommended that the individual school be given as much budgetary independence as possible. This does not reduce accountability; rather, it increases the principal's accountability to use it wisely toward the improvement of specific learning situations in the school. (pp. 201–2)

The trend toward site-based decision-making means that school officials must take on more and more budget and management duties. What must a principal know to secure and monitor the resources needed to achieve the collective vision of the learning community? How does a learning community reorder its priorities and design a budget and related resources to correspond to changing demographics, local needs, and the collective vision of the school? How do the learning community and the principal ensure that money spent will yield the maximum enhancement of learning at the classroom level? How does the principal create a budget process that involves key stakeholders representative of the learning community in financial decisions? This chapter addresses the budgetary process and the importance of engaging the participation of the learning community to develop a budget that will provide the resources necessary to improve the school's quality of life and learning.

Research shows that effective schools use their resources to support improvement activities and demonstrate good budgeting and planning practices (Ubben and Hughes 1992; Candoli, Hack, and Ray 1992). These are important lessons to remember for a learning community bent on reaching the goals of its vision. The learning community must understand the budgetary process and the extent and use of its resources and make decisions based on carrying out the vision.

There must be a clear relationship between the use of resources reflected in the budget and the priorities of the learning community.

SITE-BASED MANAGEMENT AND THE BUDGET

Today's schools operate in a complex informational society that is far different from the outdated industrial model that most school organizations follow when preparing their budgets. Recognizing this, the Educate America Act Goals 2000 (National Education Goals Panel 1993) calls for different delivery systems, resource allocations, and policies to meet a diverse student population and their multitude of learning needs. The Educate America Act advocates for service integration to ensure meeting all students' needs in a comprehensive, broad-based manner. Categorical programming, though well-intentioned, has led to fragmentation of programs and reduction of direct services to children in public schools (Fink 1992; McLaughlin and Warren 1992). To rectify this problem, researchers and policy-makers have substantiated the need to provide more decision-making power for resource allocation to educators at each school because they are most familiar with the students and their learning (Short and Greer 1997; Candoli, Hack, and Ray 1992). The fragmentation of current models for funding and ways of providing services requires substantial rethinking of school budgets.

The concerted effort of the learning community to ensure that the outlay of budget dollars meets student and classroom needs through site-based management undergirds a rethinking process. The basic idea of site-based management is to take schooling decisions away from the central office of a district and put those decisions into the hands of individual schools in the district to better meet the needs of students (Short and Greer 1997). The supposition is that the principal and staff members of a school are in a better position than district office administrators to decide what instructional arrangements are appropriate for students attending the school. The logic behind site-based management is clear, but the problem rests with the amount of autonomy a district is willing to give the school, principal, and staff in budgeting matters (Greer 1993).

Establishing a clear budgetary mechanism empowers a learning community to make crucial decisions on how and why money is spent. Site-based management means that schools within a district are allotted money to purchase supplies, equipment, personnel, utilities, maintenance, and perhaps other services according to their own assessment of what is appropriate (Ubben and Hughes 1992). Clune and White (1988) describe school-based management as a system designed to improve education by increasing the authority of actors at the school site. Similarly, the findings of effective schools research substantiate the rationale behind site-based management with the conclusion that the more closely a decision is made to a student, the more likely the decision is to serve the student better (Odden 1995).

Therefore, rethinking a school budget to meet the needs of diverse learners within a school allows for greater participation, accountability, and creativity by a principal and the rest of the learning community. However, it also means learning about site-based management and how budgets can drive appropriate programming. Odden and Picus (1992) highlight the issues in school budgeting:

> Budgeting, or the allocation of resources to achieve instructional or organizational goals, is one of the most important functions of school management. Discussions of budget theory are filled with high expectations. Hartman (1988) states that the school budget "is an important tool for school administrators to understand and utilize in achieving their basic mission—educating children in the most effective and cost-efficient manner. Unfortunately, actual budgeting practices fall far short of these high aspirations. (p. 300)

RETHINKING BUDGET DEVELOPMENT IN A LEARNING COMMUNITY

The traditional school budget has allocated funds for specific categories without a relationship to a school's goals and needs. If a learning community is to reach its goals and meet the needs of its students, the budget development process and final budget must reflect its priorities for the school. There must be a correlation between the learning community's vision, goals, and needs and how it spends its budget. A budget provides the resources for carrying out the vision of the learning community.

Consequently, in rethinking a school budget the learning community must answer a few essential questions to focus on using the budget to meet its vision, goals, and needs. Figure 9.1 provides key questions to consider in the process of rethinking and developing a budget. For a school to move from a district-mandated, categorical budgeting process to one that involves site-based management and decision-making, it must set up a budget process that will focus the learning community on its vision, goals, and needs. The principal must facilitate

- How are current resources being allocated to reach the learning community's vision?
- How does the school budget process involve the learning community in reaching its vision?
* How should budget allocations reflect the vision, goals, and needs of the learning community?

FIGURE 9.1
Rethinking a School Budget: Essential Questions

and monitor the budget process so that the learning community can see the link between the budget—how the school spends its money—and student success, which should be the outcome of budget expenses.

Raising these essential budget questions may be easier than offering solutions. Integrating special, compensatory, categorical, and general educational funds and services into a school budget model designed and managed by the learning community takes time and facilitation skills of the principal to keep the learning community focused. This is not an easy task, given the various constituencies that have historical ownership of specific areas of funding. The principal's role is to educate, facilitate, and lead the learning community to an understanding of the budget and how the parts of the budget relate with one another, always keeping a focus on the goals, needs, and vision of the school. The principal must spend time through this educational process explaining the various aspects of the budget so that the learning community understands the sources of income and how the expenditures must correlate with the key goals of the school.

Rethinking the budget starts with a conceptualization by the learning community of how to meet the instructional needs of all students through an in-depth budgetary process that reflects the learning community's vision for learning. The principal and other learning community members must develop the skills necessary to create a budgetary process. The principal must present budget data, historical budget information, and other budget information necessary to better understand the current status of the school budget. Through thoughtful review of the current budget and the school goals during budget planning meetings, the learning community can determine budgetary allocations that better meet the current needs of the school. The developed school budget should become the resource action plan for the school. The change generated by this budget process with the learning community not only benefits all students but also reduces the inefficiency of a fragmentized school budget and builds on the inclusive culture of the learning community working together for its vision.

Too often, schools make plans without any correlation to the school budget and resource allocation (Candoli, Hack, and Ray 1992). No wonder school reform languishes—the resources to drive change are misallocated or missing altogether. The principal and the rest of the learning community must understand that the budget's allocation of resources has a tremendous effect on what happens in a school. The budget drives the school's programs. Without the necessary resources, a school cannot realize its vision. This may discourage members of the school learning community when they envision change, but they will not receive the money needed to support their efforts unless they take the right steps and fully understand the budget process.

THE SITE BUDGET TEAM

A critical aspect of rethinking the school budget is the need for a shared decision-making process involving teachers, staff, parents, community members, and the principal. If this process is left to chance, little will happen beyond the first budget overview stage. Therefore, to back up the leader's good intentions, the learning community needs to form a Site Budget Team to develop and monitor the school budget and make sure it ties into the school's vision.

The Site Budget Team should consist of a group that is representative of the school learning community: teachers, principal, staff, students, parents, and other community members. This team should study all the school's known funding sources. Identifying current general funds, categorical funds, income, and expenditures can help enable the team to grasp the status of the budget's current funding and expenditures. The initial study of a school's current budget should provide each team member a clear picture of how resources are currently used: instruction, administration, maintenance, supplies, equipment, personnel, and other services.

Central to this initial process is a set of questions to help the Site Budget Team begin not only comprehending the scope and complexity of budgeting but also "owning" the process (see Figure 9.2). The adage, "knowledge is power," applies concretely to a budget process. By using these budget questions, the Site Budget Team can clarify the budget process and the team's role in preparing, monitoring, and revising the school budget.

What Questions Should be Asked About the Site Budget Process?

- What is the school's vision, and how does the current budget reflect that vision?
- Who makes budget decisions at the site level?
- How has the budget been traditionally allocated?
- What have other restructuring schools done with their budgets?
- How flexible will the district office and the board of education be with a new budget procedure and allocations?
- How will the principal support the work of the Site Budget Team?
- How will school staff members react to a review of budget allocations, including staffing positions?
- What type of training and coaching will the Site Budget Team require?
- How does the school provide for accountability of a budget tied to student outcomes?
- What type of waivers will be needed from state and federal agencies to carry out the budget plans and the use of categorical budgets?
- How will all members of the learning community be kept informed of the budget development process, and how will they have input?

FIGURE 9.2
Budget Questions: Understanding the Process

After answering the budget questions about the general budget process, the Site Budget Team must address specific questions for analyzing the site budget as a follow-up to the initial questions (see Figure 9.3). These specific questions provide the Site Budget Team with valuable information about allocations formulas and needed expenditures and raise issues for long-term budget planning and maintenance for a learning community.

After answering the questions in Figure 9.3, the Site Budget Team should have a clearer understanding of the school budget to use as the basis to begin writing a budget that reflects the learning community's vision.

Additional budget training for the Site Budget Team would provide an opportunity for members to think more creatively about how to use the present budget resources to provide for an improved educational program. Since most members of the team will be novices regarding budget planning, resource allocation, and accounting procedures, the principal initially should educate, coach, and assist the team with its work. Once the team acquires a basic understanding of the budget process, they should begin the work of designing the school budget. This highly involved and convoluted task is made yet harder by the traditional budget and special categorical program mindsets of teachers, staff, parents, and the funding regulations of state and federal programs. The Site Budget Team's careful study and development of the school budget can provide for a clear focus based on the vision.

Site-based budgeting requires increased involvement at the local school level along with a long-term plan—three to five years. The Site Budget Team must be aware of changing demographics and project

---

- What is the unit budget? ($ x student enrollment, or what is the district formula for allocations?)
- What instructional funds does the school receive?
- What categorical funds does the school receive?
    Special Education
    School Improvement Program
    Chapter 1 and 2
    Title 7
    Economic Impact Aid
    Vocational Education Act
    Co-Curricular
    Counseling
    Drug, Alcohol, and Tobacco Education
    Grants
    Limited English Proficiency Program
    Other (Check with other principals and district office)
- What funds does the school receive for professional development of staff, including substitute funds?
- What funds are received for furniture and replacement of equipment?
- What funds are received to purchase new equipment?
- Who funds maintenance items, such as rugs, painting, and so forth?
- Who funds the repair of computers and audiovisual equipment?
- Who funds the cost of postage?
- Who funds the cost of making copies?
- Who funds building maintenance, capital improvements, and maintenance of the school grounds?
- Who receives the funds for building usage by outside groups?
- Who funds custodial services for special events?
- What have the site expenditures in the school budget been over the last five years?

FIGURE 9.3
Budget Questions: Analyzing the Site Budget

how those demographics will change five years or more into the future. This is foreign to the tradition-bound school district that has always based its planning on year-long fiscal cycles. However, integrating demographic information with changing student needs will allow the team to develop a budget for the coming year and establish budget priorities for several years ahead. From a fiscal management standpoint, the practices of anticipating trends and making necessary adjustments reflect sound judgment. A Site Budget Team that forecasts instructional needs could obtain resources from other sources, such as private foundation grants and projects, and target those resources at improving student learning to reach the learning community's vision.

BUDGET PROCESS FOR THE SITE BUDGET TEAM

The budget process for a Site Budget Team involves sequential steps that are cyclical each year. Figure 9.4 shows these steps: reviewing the school vision, goals, and needs; planning and allocating money; considering, modifying, and adopting the final budget; managing the budget, which includes record keeping; and reviewing and evaluating yearly budget activities.

According to Ubben and Hughes (1992), the budget process should be continuous and cyclical; the final step of review and appraisal immediately precedes the next cycle of budgeting. It permits responsible financial planning for the school, based on the Site Budget

FIGURE 9.4
Overview of the Budget Process

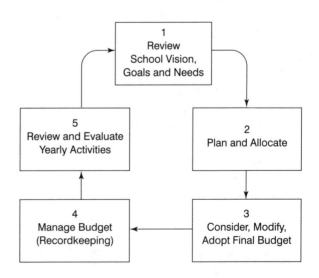

Team's review of budget data and the connection between spending and fulfilling the school vision. The principal is fiscally responsible for the daily implementation of the budget's allocation, but the Site Budget Team provides the fundamental direction, planning, and allocation of the money. The learning community must be able to see the connection between what it aims for and the use of funds to support efforts to reach those aims. Good budgeting is the result of careful planning and financial resourcefulness (Ubben and Hughes 1992).

REVIEWING AND PLANNING

Educational planning, the weighing of priorities and of alternative means to accomplish them, is the essential feature of budgeting in the schools. (Candoli, Hack, and Ray 1992, 111)

Essential to the success of the Site Budget Team is an initial planning orientation meeting wherein team members become acquainted with budget data and the significance of their role in the budget process. This initial meeting should provide team members the time to discuss crucial site-budget issues and how those issues affect the budget's development and implementation. It is well worth the time to think about how a budget can drive instruction as well as align itself with the values and needs of teachers, students, and the rest of the learning community.

To begin, the Site Budget Team should consider how the budget affects the following key concepts in planning the budget:

- The school's vision and mission
- The school's plan including goals and objectives
- Student expectations and achievement
- Parent expectations
- School and community values and needs

Reviewing these key concepts gives Site Budget Team members a chance to explore their feelings and thoughts on how budgets influence the school. As Candoli, Hack, and Ray (1992) describe it:

The school budget is basically an instrument of educational planning and, incidentally, an instrument of control. It reflects the organizational pattern by categorizing the elements of a total plan. . . . Budgeting, then, forces the community, administrators, and staff to plan together what needs to be done, how it will be done, and by whom it will be done. (p. 111)

The Steps in the Site Budget Team Process (see Figure 9.5) consist of phases, giving a sense of the scope and sequence of the budget process. This illustration elaborates on the five phases depicted in the overview in Figure 9.4.

The principal and a representative from the district business office should present pertinent data and regulations about the school budget to the Site Budget Team so that all team members have a realistic picture of the budget. The Site Budget Team members should explore reasons why the site budget has traditionally allocated funds in a certain manner. Do any regulations inhibit creativity? Are there direct links between allocation of resources and student learning? Is student achievement tied to the school budget? These are pertinent questions to the budget process. Site Budget Team members should realize the importance of their role in determining fiscal accountability and how the budget ties into increased success for students. Through critical analysis of the site budget, team members can begin to define the directions they may propose with the budget. The budget process should help drive efforts to achieve the school's vision through change and improvement.

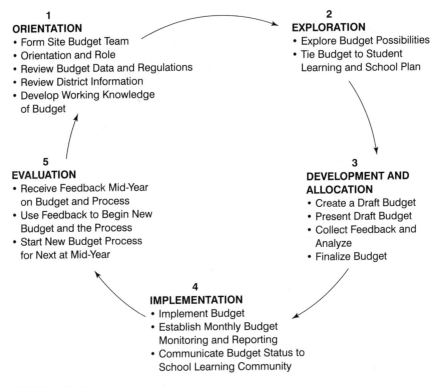

1
ORIENTATION
- Form Site Budget Team
- Orientation and Role
- Review Budget Data and Regulations
- Review District Information
- Develop Working Knowledge of Budget

2
EXPLORATION
- Explore Budget Possibilities
- Tie Budget to Student Learning and School Plan

5
EVALUATION
- Receive Feedback Mid-Year on Budget and Process
- Use Feedback to Begin New Budget and the Process
- Start New Budget Process for Next at Mid-Year

3
DEVELOPMENT AND ALLOCATION
- Create a Draft Budget
- Present Draft Budget
- Collect Feedback and Analyze
- Finalize Budget

4
IMPLEMENTATION
- Implement Budget
- Establish Monthly Budget Monitoring and Reporting
- Communicate Budget Status to School Learning Community

FIGURE 9.5
Steps in the Site Budget Team Process

Allowing for flexible, creative ways of managing resources at the local school level will undoubtedly affect the classroom. The Site Budget Team has the ability to ask powerful questions about the funding of school programs, with the goal of bringing about change and better education for students.

Clarifying questions and studying the budget information over several meetings can provide a baseline of information for team members to make decisions. Gathering information and having a clear understanding of categorical programs empowers the team to review the budget. Specific questions must be asked about regulations on budget expenditures, tracking of expenditures, and possible waivers to use general or categorical funds. Through this process, team members develop a working knowledge of the current budget and gain information on how the budget might be reworked to provide the best coordinated services for all students.

CONSIDERING, MODIFYING, AND ADOPTING THE BUDGET

After completing their study and questioning of current site and district budget practices, the team should formulate a tentative budget. Knowledge derived from the planning meeting creates a framework for the team to entertain new options. Along the way, team members should apprise the learning community of their progress on the budget. All team members should establish clear communication channels to allay any fears that others in the school may have about the budget process. Informing various stakeholders can avert problems, in part by providing those outside the budget team an opportunity to voice their concerns and desires and thus participate in writing the budget.

When team members are satisfied with the draft budget, they should distribute it to all stakeholder groups for information, feedback, and analysis. It may be necessary to hold several meetings with stakeholders to address and consider their concerns. Absent such consideration, problems may arise during implementation of the budget. After securing stakeholder feedback and analysis, the team can make the necessary changes.

After making modifications, the Site Budget Team should finalize and present the budget to all stakeholders in the learning community. Team members should encourage continuous, open communication with the stakeholders via formal and informal meetings and other lines of communication to monitor the new budgetary process. If team members fail to establish open communication at this stage, ill feelings over allocations and priorities may develop and overshadow the team's work up to this point.

After approval of the budget, the Site Budget Team along with the principal should implement the budget exactly as prescribed. Deviating from the approved plan would reduce the credibility of the team. If budget problems should occur, the team must solve them collectively and openly. In essence, opening up the budget process in these ways should help all stakeholders understand and take ownership of their learning community's budget.

MANAGING THE BUDGET

Throughout the year, the Site Budget Team should implement and review the budget, analyzing monthly budget monitoring information and scheduling monthly meetings to communicate progress on the new budget. The principal is responsible for the budget's day-to-day management, coordination, and record keeping. The team members must share monthly budget information with their constituents to keep the entire learning community informed about progress on implementing the budget. The team should present a midyear report on the budget, including highlights from the current year and proposed recommendations for the next budget year. This report will inform members of the learning community, who can then provide feedback that the team can use to begin the budget process for the next year.

REVIEWING AND EVALUATING THE YEARLY BUDGET

Planning for review of the next year's budget should begin no later than January to ensure adequate time to discuss all budgetary issues and anticipate the impact of any district, state, and national changes on school budgets. All members of the learning community should have access to a copy of the budget summary so they can review the budget, suggest changes, and provide other input. Also, team members might consider preparing an overview of the spending of funds throughout the year, which they could publish in a newsletter or otherwise make available to the learning community. Communicating in this way means that not only stakeholders at the school but also members of the community outside the school can more readily perceive and understand fiscal accountability. A yearly budget evaluation can give the Site Budget

Team time to review and provide for accountability for budget allocations and expenditures as they relate to the school's vision.

SUMMARY

Given the decision-making power to use funds for instructional programs, the Site Budget Team becomes the accountability team to ensure the intertwining of resources and student learning. When members of the learning community work together to determine how they can fund instructional programs to meet the needs of a diverse student population, the budget process can evolve into a method of empowering all members. Members of the Site Budget Team are aware that they have limited resources and must provide a focus for the school budget to bring about the changes necessary to improve and support student achievement.

Site-based management generates more opportunities to solve complex problems. It provides a needed forum for new teachers and maturing professionals to work together toward common agendas. To that end, the Site Budget Team process incorporates the best principles of participatory management—for stakeholders at the local school level truly make decisions affecting the lives of children. The principal must ensure that the budget process and outcomes address the overall learning community's vision.

REFLECTIVE ACTIVITIES

1. Analyzing a School's Budget

Review a school's budget using the budget questions (Figure 9.2) in this chapter. What insights have you gained about budget analysis?

2. Using the Budget Process

Use the steps in the Site Budget Team Process (Figure 9.5) to review a school's budget process. What did you learn about the budget process? What changes would you suggest after this review?

3. Interview a Principal About the Budget

Interview a school principal about the budget process. What insights did you gain? How do the principal's ideas about the school budget process relate to the issues raised in this chapter about setting up a Site Budget Team and reaching the learning community's vision?

SUGGESTED READINGS

Candoli, Carl, Walter G. Hack, and John R. Ray. 1992. *School Business Administration: A Planning Approach*. Boston: Allyn and Bacon.

Odden, Allen R., and Lawrence O. Picus. 1992. *School Finance: A Policy Perspective*. New York: McGraw-Hill.

Short, Paula M., and John T. Greer. 1997. *Leadership in Empowered Schools: Themes from Innovative Efforts*. Upper Saddle River, NJ: Merrill/Prentice Hall.

Ubben, Gerald, and Larry W. Hughes. 1992. *The Principal: Creative Leadership for Effective Schools*. Boston: Allyn and Bacon.

REFERENCES

Candoli, Carl, Walter G. Hack, and John R. Ray. 1992. *School Business Administration: A Planning Approach*. Boston: Allyn and Bacon.

Clune, William, and Paula White. 1988. *School-Based Management: Institutional Variation, Implementation, and Issues for Further Research*. New Brunswick, NJ: Rutgers University, Center for Policy Research in Education.

Drake, Thelbert L., and William H. Roe. 1994. *The Principalship*, 4th ed. Upper Saddle River, NJ: Merrill/Prentice Hall.

Fink, Stephen. 1992. How We Restructured Our Categorical Program. *Educational Leadership* 50(2): 42–43.

Greer, John. 1993. *The Autonomous School*. Paper presented at the annual meeting of the National Council of Professors of Educational Administration, Indian Wells, CA.

Hartman, William T. 1988. *School District Budgeting*. Englewood Cliffs, NJ: Prentice Hall.

McLaughlin, Milbrey W., and Sandra H. Warren. 1992. *Issues and Options in Restructuring Schools and Special Education Programs.* Reston, VA: Council of Exceptional Children.

National Education Goals Panel. 1993. National Education Goals Report: Building a Nation of Learners. Washington, DC: National Education Goals Panel.

Odden, Allan R. 1995. *Educational Leadership for America's Schools.* New York: McGraw-Hill.

Odden, Allan R., and Lawrence O. Picus. 1992. *School Finance: A Policy Perspective.* New York: McGraw-Hill.

Short, Paula M., and John T. Greer. 1997. *Leadership in Empowered Schools: Themes from Innovative Efforts.* Upper Saddle River, NJ: Merrill/Prentice Hall.

Ubben, Gerald, and Larry W. Hughes. 1992. *The Principal: Creative Leadership for Effective Schools.* Boston: Allyn and Bacon.

CHAPTER 10

USE OF TECHNOLOGY

Technology's Impact on the School and the Principal

Definition of Technology

Technology Planning

PROBLEM SCENARIO

Y ou, the principal, are approached by a group of parents who want to see more computers and related innovations in your school. What is your vision for the role of technology in your school? Do your teachers and staff share that vision, or has planning been helter-skelter? How will technology support your school's instruction and administration? How does your school prepare students for the technological age and beyond? Can teachers, students, and administrators use the Internet, the World Wide Web, and other such tools to access and process information?

TECHNOLOGY'S IMPACT ON THE SCHOOL AND THE PRINCIPAL

If the mission of a learning community places priority on educating the whole child, then the significance of what the school does regarding new technology increases as it approaches the twenty-first century. Such telecommunications modes as e-mail, fax, voice mail, interactive video, the Internet, and the World Wide Web have made the world smaller and vast amounts of information more accessible. It is essential, therefore, that all students develop the necessary skills, values, and opportunities to become successful citizens in a highly technological and competitive modern world. Goal 6 of the National Education Goals 2000 (*Data for The National Education Goals Report* 1995) emphasizes the importance of preparing students in this way:

Goal 6: Adult Literacy and Lifelong Learning
By the year 2000, every adult American will be literate and will possess the knowledge and skills necessary to compete in a global economy and exercise the rights and responsibilities of citizenship.

Objective 2: All workers will have the opportunity to acquire the knowledge and skills, from basic to highly technical, needed to adapt to emerging new technologies, work methods, and markets through public and private educational, vocational, technical, workplace, or other programs. (p. 93)

Goals 2000 (*Data for the National Education Goals Report* 1995) further emphasizes the importance of lifelong learning for every learning community and the nation as a whole:

Lifelong learning has never been more important. With the speed and scope of change taking place around the world, the skills needed to be an effective worker and citizen are rapidly increasing in complexity. To survive and prosper, Americans must choose to value and invest in continued learning. Any other choice has serious consequences for individuals and for society itself. (p. 92)

Thus technology is a key tool in building a learning community within a school. As a leader and facilitator for the learning community, the principal must understand the importance of keeping abreast of technological change. Technology provides vital links among individuals, schools, and other organizations; manages and accesses information that enables interaction; and allows learning to take place in new and dynamic ways. Technology releases individual learners, classroom teachers, staff members, administrators, and the school from an outdated reliance on textbook and paper. It opens them up to interactive learning, instant access to timely information, and a means to communicate and learn in different media. These numerous opportunities for learning make it critical for the learning community, including the principal, to understand new technology. Most learning communities, however, are just beginning to develop, understand, and utilize new technology.

Many forces now push for integrating new technologies into the schools. Parents worry about whether their children's skills in the new technologies—especially computers—will fully prepare them to enter the workforce. Businesses are emphasizing computer and technological literacy. As an example of these efforts, Weiler (1988) cites the California Business Round Table Report, which recommended enabling all schools to integrate technology with instruction and management. The basis for this recommendation is the belief that educational technologies can revolutionize teaching and learning, improve achievement, motivate students, and make learning more exciting and accessible to different kinds of learners. New technology holds out the possibility of very different, more productive roles for teachers, freeing them from time they traditionally spend on bookkeeping tasks and instruction based on textbooks. The report called for new information systems and well-designed instructional modules to give students access to multimedia learning resources. Foundations have also emphasized the use and integration of new technologies into schools. Many foundation grants reflect the need for technological literacy, awarding money to encourage schools to teach the requisite skills. Computer businesses have set up some of the largest foundations to award grants to carry out such work. Among them are Hewlett-Packard, Intel/Noyce, Apple, and IBM.

The issue of the role of technology in education is reflected in an ongoing national debate. In "Moving Technology into Education: Is It a Fit?" Zimmerman (1992) points out:

> From Goals 2000 to state legislatures to local PTA meetings, people persuaded in large part by the high-tech industry itself herald technology as the savior of American education. A related argument holds that if today's students are to be adequately prepared for work, they must be "computer literate." (p. 2)

Thus, the promise of advanced technology is enormous, as is the push toward the use of that technology. Various local, state, and national reports and initiatives have put new technologies and technological literacy on school agendas. School restructuring efforts at all levels further echo the need for increased teaching of state-of-the-art technology. A principal must understand the promise of new technology as well as the problems it can raise for a school.

Many scholars see the tools of technology as ways to obtain the skills of acquiring, managing, thinking about, and using information. Willis, Thomas, and Hoppe (1985) state that new technology is changing the way we perceive our world. They are quick to point out, however, that our schools remain tied to the print-dominated age and our teaching styles remain captive to print technology. The wide gap between the technological tools available to schools and the number of teachers who understand and use them effectively is apparent in schools (Murray and Murray 1994). In some cases, traditional teaching methods are at odds with today's visual and interactive technology methods.

The principal's understanding of the many facets of technology is critical as schools prepare students for the twenty-first century. Developing a true sense of a learning community that uses technology to advance learning is important. To help the principal understand technology, this chapter covers three aspects of technology—planning for technology, technology in instruction, and technology in administration—as related to the principalship and building a learning community. Murray and Murray (1994) emphasize the importance of understanding technology and its uses in schools:

> Our children are truly children of an electronic age. We need to view technology from a total perspective. It is not enough to simply view the instruction of technology as the training of students on the use of technological devices. We as educators need to establish new working principles that will guide our growth and address the nature and impact of technology on the teaching and learning process. (p. 192)

Thus, it is important for a principal and others in the learning community to understand the many aspects of technology for enriching learning and managing school affairs as well as to grasp the problems and liabilities implementing new technology can bring. The learning community must continue to learn about new technology and learn through it.

DEFINITION OF TECHNOLOGY

What is meant by technology? It is more than the use of computers. The technological tools available today span a wide variety of devices that provide effective media to many instructional and administrative activities.

The term **technology** as used in this chapter refers to the multifaceted use of electronic equipment including computers and peripheral equipment, such as CD-ROMs, laser disks, printers, servers, and modems; television; video cameras and recorders; telecommunications links, including e-mail, fax, teleconferencing, the Internet, and the World Wide Web; and other emerging technologies. In schools, technology is generally viewed as an instructional or administrative tool that individuals use to enhance, transform, and help learning for all students.

A 1970 report to the president and Congress, *To Improving Learning*, provided a definition of instructional technology that still applies today (Committee on Instructional Technology 1970):

> Instructional technology goes beyond any particular medium or device. In this sense, instructional technology is more than the sum of its parts. It is a systematic way of designing, carrying out,

and evaluating the total process of learning and teaching in terms of specific objectives, based upon research in human learning and communications, and employing a combination of human and non-human resources to bring about more effective instruction. (p. 5)

As it applies to today's schools, this definition implies that educators must systematically make thoughtful decisions on how to apply technology to establish a learning climate, direct their instructional environment, and plan learning and improved instructional experiences. Heinich et al. (1996) further emphasize the importance of the decision-making process for administrators and teachers as a means for planning instruction for the information age, which includes various learning styles and a multiple intelligences perspective that meets the needs of most students. If used simply to automate traditional methods of teaching and learning, technology will have little impact on schools. Using technology to introduce new ways of teaching and learning will have a major impact, especially practices that extend beyond the walls of the school into the community, the workplace, and the family (O'Neil 1995).

Employing new technology in administration and management includes various means to enhance the accessing, processing, and evaluating of data and resources to make the school run as efficiently and effectively as possible. Principals can take advantage of these benefits of new technology to find more efficient methods of managing their schools.

TECHNOLOGY PLANNING

Figure 10.1 shows key areas that school officials must address as they prepare to teach and use new technology: forming the vision; setting up planning; determining instruction uses; ensuring access and equity; implementing budgets, acquisitions, and maintenance; clarifying administration; creating professional development; analyzing configurations; carrying out implementation; and developing review, evaluation, and revision processes (Barnett 1995; Dowell and Raffel 1994; Murray and Murray 1994; Knapp and Glenn 1996; CSDOE 1994). These topics form the organization for the rest of this chapter. Each topic will be discussed with implications that a learning community and principal need to consider in their school's technology planning.

FIRST THE VISION, THEN THE TECHNOLOGY

Before the planning starts, the learning community must settle on a common vision of technology's role in education. Though the vision

FIGURE 10.1
Technology Planning

District and School Areas to Address:

- Vision
- Planning
- Instructional uses
- Access and equity
- Budgeting, acquisition, and maintenance
- Administrative uses
- Professional development
- Configurations
- Implementation
- Evaluation and revision

compact or agreement may be slow in emerging, it is key to understanding the purpose and uses of technology. The technology must be viewed as a means of empowering students to learn and teachers to teach. Schools must employ technological innovations in ways that reinforce and help fulfill the vision of the learning community (Knapp and Glenn 1996).

Technology tools become useful as they are applied to educational tasks, not merely as inanimate teaching machines. An important distinction is the open-ended use of software such as word processing, computer-aided drawing, or hypertext markup language programs to enable students to explore, organize, and create rather than using software to manage students. The student must manage the computer—not the other way around—to learn to solve open-ended problems. A nationwide survey found that 95 percent of computers in grades K–12 use so-called educational software either to replace teaching or help students practice content (Zimmerman 1992, 3). Using new technology in such a way—to manage students—wastes the promise of scientific advances and discards the chance to improve education. The learning community must use new technology to support its collective vision, not manage students.

The pressure to make students computer-literate can be intense. Many schools give in to the pressure for technology but do not buy into a vision of technology for the school. Often a showcase, stand-alone laboratory is staffed by an aide or parent volunteers as a solution to technology needs. There usually is little effort to mesh lab work with classroom curriculum. Researchers have noted that students who use computer labs are likely to learn about technology instead of learning with it (Zimmerman 1992; Knapp and Glenn 1996). Integrate computers into the classroom and curriculum, and students learn with as well as about technology. With computers in the regular classroom, students engage in intellectual exercise, pick up specific content, and develop computer literacy all at the same time. Teachers should use technology to supplement and reinforce what they are already doing in the classroom, not replace it (Zimmerman 1992).

Technology's greatest educational potential is its power to create equal and immediate access to information and expertise. But even with this great potential for technology's uses, an innovation is only as beneficial as the teacher's ability to help students develop investigative, analytic, and managerial skills to build context and meaning for information. Principals must help teachers—as well as themselves—understand the teaching potentials of technology and explore the possibilities of technology.

As Zimmerman (1992) and Knapp and Glenn (1996) warn, some technology is so user-friendly that students may be tempted to spend most of their time fiddling with format, expending substantially less effort on content. Teachers must help students balance substance and image, making sure that students involve themselves in the content and not just the technology. Principals can help teachers monitor these types of problems and make adjustments as needed, helping students refocus on engaging with the content and using technology as a means to access content.

School reform groups such as the Coalition of Essential Schools are enthusiastic about technology but have tempered their enthusiasm with pragmatism (Cushman 1994):

> Rather than put the technological cart before the horse of classroom change, they warn, schools must first focus on what their core issues are—then use technology wisely in devising new approaches. When essential schools plan backwards from their goals, they see technology as a tool, not an end. (p. 1)

How quickly should educators and principals embrace new technology that often proves obsolete in a short time? How can educators, including principals, create a synergy between new technology and restructuring schools, using one to bolster and inspire the other? How can technology focus on getting students to use their minds well? The learning community must discuss these matters before settling on a technology plan for the school.

Cushman (1994) in *Horace*, the Coalition of Essential Schools newsletter, makes an important point about how technology can support a school's goals and vision:

> No matter how powerful, high tech alone can't make schools better. But if schools will first define the issues facing them, technology can prove a key strategy in achieving their goals. (p. 1)

PLANNING

A principal who understands technology planning and its relationship to instruction and administration can guide the learning community as it seeks to use technology to increase student achievement. Such a principal understands that planning affords learning community members the opportunity to discuss, decide, implement, and evaluate technology's role. The resultant dialogue can spur growth in the learning community as the sharing of ideas helps the community evolve and institute new uses of technology.

The principal must begin the school's technology planning with a discussion of assumptions about technology. A consensus on the issues will provide direction to the technology plan and also save many hours. Barnett (1995) provides an example of technology assumptions developed by the Cupertino Union School District in California for planning technology (see Figure 10.2).

The learning community must create clear assumptions for the study of various aspects of technology to set the direction for technology planning. Together the principal and the rest of the learning community must find a direction based on their beliefs about what technology can offer education. Zimmerman (1992) warns of the concerns with technology and the lack of vision for its use in education:

> Technology has something to offer education; they're just not sure what. For all the excitement and the millions of dollars already spent on technology in the schools, still missing is a guiding vision about how it can or should be used to further classroom education. Even now some schools buy a raft of computers and then try to figure out how to use them. (p. 2)

Planning Technology—Successful Strategies

- Technology use will increase productivity—productivity means outcomes and efficiency.

- Effective technology use demands district top-down planning and school-based bottom-up implementation.

- A clear strategic educational vision must determine technology use.

- Technology in schools must be central to, not supplementary to, the educational enterprise.

- All three phases of the integration process—planning, implementation and ongoing management—must be managed for effective outcomes.

FIGURE 10.2
An Example of Technology Assumptions

Educators and administrators must look at what research says about technology's impact on learning and the school and understand trends in technology to avoid heading down a low-tech, dead-end road for education. Formulating and setting up effective programs to teach about new technology requires getting solid information on how various approaches affect education. Lack of information has left many schools with little more than outdated hardware and poorly educated students. Learning communities, which are notoriously strapped for cash, cannot afford to waste their precious resources trying to implement high-tech plans that are based on insufficient data.

The technology plan must address curriculum and instructional needs, current resources, where the school wants to be, and what is needed to get there. Specific topics include hardware, software related to curriculum, professional development to promote the use of advanced technological tools, staff requirements, and research (Murray and Murray 1994, 195). In addition, the plan must address maintenance and security.

A technology committee formed by the principal can provide a representative voice (teachers, staff members, students, parents, etc.) for the learning community in developing a three- to five-year plan. Developing the initial plan is only the first step of the committee's work. The committee must remain intact for several years after finishing the initial plan and continue to revisit, revise, and refocus the technology plan as resources, insights, and needs change (Murray and Murray 1994). Subcommittees can focus on specific areas throughout the process of creating, implementing, and revising the technology plan. The technology plan, with the help of a technology committee, must become a living document for the learning community's vision for technology in the school. The principal's role should be to facilitate and monitor the technology committee's ongoing work.

Technology that enhances education requires detailed planning involving teachers, the principal, staff members, the district, other community members, and sometimes students, and its use must be targeted directly at educational goals. In an evaluation of technology programs at several California schools, Cradler (cited in Zimmerman 1992) found that with detailed planning, teachers worked harder at integrating technology in support of curricular goals. The author also reported that student achievement improved and that students had better study skills, more self-confidence, and more initiative. Cradler concluded that without planning, technology remained incidental, adding little to the quality of education in the school.

Districts and schools must make a long-term commitment to combining technology with educational programs and planning, making it an integral part of the school system. In providing assistance with planning for technology initiatives, districts and schools can use outside experts to provide direct support to classrooms and schools. The experts can help ensure that computing and other forms of technology become part of the school's daily instruction and operations. Further, experts can train teachers and other staff members to help train their peers as they become confident and proficient in using advanced technology (Murray and Murray 1994, 196).

The district plays a key role in technology planning and efficient use of resources for both instruction and management. Technology planning, support, training, and maintenance at the district level are essential parts of a school's technology planning and implementation. The school technology committee must make sure its plans are compatible with the district's technology plans and expectations. Coordination of efforts throughout a district can help schools develop technology usage that is consistent both in instruction and management.

REFLECTIONS: AS A NEW PRINCIPAL AND GIVEN YOUR EXPERI-

ENCES AS A TEACHER, WHAT ARE THE ISSUES YOU WOULD SEE

FOR PLANNING TECHNOLOGY IN YOUR SCHOOL? WRITE DOWN

YOUR THOUGHTS.

INSTRUCTIONAL USES OF TECHNOLOGY

The instructional implications of technology are mind-boggling because it can free students from the constraints of learning from a single textbook and extend the school library beyond its physical walls. The use of information technology can become a learning process itself not only for students, but also for teachers and staff as they stretch their knowledge by exploring its expanding nature.

Computer-assisted instruction has been around for many years, but generally in limited ways, such as helping students gain rudimentary skills through rote techniques. While this type of instruction still exists in schools, most restructuring schools envision more creative and interactive approaches with computers and technology. Student research and writing projects use such programs as Apple's HyperCard and IBM's Linkway as well as video, CD-ROM, and laser disk technologies. Restructuring schools are investing heavily in technologies to support new avenues of teaching and learning (Dowell and Raffel 1994, 231). Students can use a variety of technologies to complete core assignments, keep digital portfolios of work, communicate, and network with other students and the community.

Regarding a project in Stevens Creek Elementary School in California, Apple Classrooms of Tomorrow (ACOT 1993) concludes:

> More than a decade ago when technology was first introduced to schools, educators and the public expected technology to launch a revolution. As we've learned, it takes more than technology to improve education. The entire system cries out for change.
>
> But technology is part of that necessary, systemic change because it profoundly disturbs the inertia of traditional classrooms. It encourages different interactions between students and teachers. Technology engages students in learning processes that develop higher communication, analysis, and problem-solving skills. Integrating technology into instruction makes teachers question their beliefs about instruction and assessment.
>
> We believe that these systemic changes enable ACOT students to better cope with change and to face the challenges of the coming century in ways many of their peers cannot. (p. 4)

Technology's impact on curriculum should be to support a student-centered, activity-oriented learning program. Through state-of-the-art technology and curriculum planning, teachers can provide student projects; students can create portfolios; and students can learn computer literacy, technological skills, and a variety of reasoning skills in an interdisciplinary manner. Teachers and principals should want students to know how to use computers as tools to access information in addition to becoming familiar with the inner workings of the hardware and software. Cushman (1994) quotes a principal who explained:

> We want students to learn! The computer and technology are tools to be used in learning. Accessing information, handling it in different ways, and communicating thoughts provides [sic] the students with a means to continued intellectual development. (p. 2)

The Coalition of Essential Schools' governing metaphor of **student as worker**, which asks students to learn how to learn with their teachers as coaches, meshes with the potential uses of technology in instruction. A profound shift in pedagogy often seems to take place in a necessary and logical manner when schools open up to technology and unlimited access to information (Cushman 1994, 2). Electronic tools are ideally suited to individual and small-group work, whether that means discussion generated by role-playing computer software, a student's video documentary presented as a course-level exhibition, or a solo research project using on-line university library sources. Communicating though e-mail with students in other schools, states, nations and collaborating nationwide on scientific databases documenting projects, such as the National Geographic Society Kids Net, are examples of the variety of opportunities that technological change offers students and teachers (Bradsher and Hagen 1995). Further, new technology can help challenge students with widely different academic backgrounds.

Murray and Murray (1994) explain that because of the use of information technology, the teacher's role will have to extend beyond disseminating information to becoming a manager of instructional resources and learning activities. The authors further state that teachers will be asked to develop expertise in diagnostic techniques, prescriptive instructional systems, development of activities and events, and assessing student achievement. Teachers will be designing more small-group instructional activities with technological applications. Working with other teachers to upgrade skills and techniques to incorporate technological skills in the classroom must become commonplace.

Technology can make learning more authentic and meaningful. An example is the Coalition of Essential Schools, which is striving to end the professional isolation of teachers, reach and challenge kids at very different levels, and assess student progress in rich and concrete ways—all things that technology can help achieve (Cushman 1994). Information technology opens students' work up to other viewers and encourages teachers to broaden their assessments to include a range of learning styles. Cushman points out that schools are using digital portfolios to document and assess student progress in a form that many people can witness and evaluate. This type of portfolio, stored on disks or CDs, can follow a student's progress with any combination of text, still pictures, audio, and video throughout the child's school career.

A few schools are realizing the possibilities of advanced information technologies and the direct intertwining of a multicultural and global curriculum (Dowell and Raffel 1994). Technology provides satellite hookups, distance learning, and networking with students elsewhere to gain a better understanding of the world and what it means to be a world citizen.

Dowell and Raffel (1994) note that teachers who want to instruct students about multiculturalism have wonderful resources besides technology skills:

> For teachers from cultures, languages, and races different from their students, computer technologies and the access to a wealth of information can be powerful. Technology carries with it the promise of expanding the capacity of the school to teach a much fuller array of knowledge and human experience in response to student inquiry. The opportunity to access databases beyond the

school site, to capture and store student research based on their own communities and lives, and to process a wide breadth of answers to questions generated by diverse students, all add immeasurably to the capacity of schools to provide meaningful multicultural curriculum. (p. 228)

The school can help parents support their child's education by establishing programs for computer loans and parent technology education classes. These types of programs can promote the development of computer literacy as well as general literacy and gain parental involvement. The use of multilanguage programs can access information for non-English speaking students and parents. An example is CLAVES (Computer Literacy Acquisition Via Educational Strategies) at Carr Intermediate School in Santa Ana, California, a program designed to improve and accelerate students' learning of English and access to new subject matter while developing new processing skills (Dowell and Raffel 1994). It provides technological skills across languages, computer literacy through the use of primary language in the content areas, and English language development experiences. These programs give students multiple ways to learn and improve their English by trying to reach each student's need and reinforce learning a new language with the parent. Thus, technology can provide a variety of learning experiences for students and ease the task of preparing to meet all students' needs by one teacher.

Instruction should be the heart of technology use within the learning community. Dowell and Raffel (1994) discuss the importance of technology in instruction:

Electronic technologies are opening the potential for new pedagogical approaches—greater flexibility, greater individualization, greater student independence, etc. This is important as students become the directors of their own learning—allowing them to build upon their own knowledge base. (p. 228)

As schools reexamine teaching and learning, the new uses of technology are being considered as are the effects. A multisensory approach to teaching by integrating technology (hardware, software, books, audiotapes, videos, etc.) allows students to learn in an engaging, interactive environment that gives them control over their own learning. By using a variety of technology and software, students can learn in the ways most natural to their individual learning styles. Educational technology is a valuable tool to improve and expand instruction to meet the evolving needs of the diverse student population, the ultimate goal for teachers. Technology offers benefits to students at all levels of ability and in all geographic regions at every level of education. Technology can help reach students and assess their progress in a variety of ways (Cushman 1994, 1). The challenge for teachers and the principal is to find ways to use technology to match individual learners with appropriate subject matter at the right level, presented in a compatible medium at an appropriate pace and in the most meaningful sequence for the student to achieve. A fundamental question is: How can technology instruction focus on getting all students to use their minds well?

The ACOT study and others suggest that integrating technology requires attention to six variables—hardware, software, staff development, curriculum, instruction, and assessment—for a technology plan to improve education significantly (Dwyer, Ringstaff, and Sandholtz 1991). Unfortunately, most districts and schools focus on hardware acquisitions almost exclusively. The extensive ACOT study of schools' computer use found that teachers took quite a while to change their approach to teaching. Further, Collins (1991) identified eight major shifts in instructional methods that often accompany extensive use of computers:

1. A shift from whole-class to small-group instruction.

2. A shift from lecture and recitation to coaching.

3. A shift from working with better students to working with weaker students.

4. A shift towards more engaged students.

5. A shift from assessment based on test performance to assessment based on products, progress, and effort.

6. A shift from a competitive to a cooperative social structure.

7. A shift from all students learning the same things to different students learning different things.

8. A shift from the primacy of verbal thinking to the integration of visual and verbal thinking. (p. 29)

ACCESS AND EQUITY

Students must have equitable access to advanced technology as they become more the directors of their learning, attempting to build on their own knowledge base. Access, equity, and preparation to use technology are particularly important for children who do not have a computer at home. Dowell and Raffel (1994) emphasize the need for access and equity:

> To address concerns regarding equal access, as well as concerns about preparation for a twenty-first century workforce, schools must design technology plans which consider equity. (p. 228)

The issues of the diverse learning needs of students and access to technology reach to the heart of a school's vision. Dowell and Raffel (1994) raise the issues, writing:

> As innovative and exciting as technology is, in most schools we visited, LEP [Limited English Proficient] students are almost wholly excluded from the emphasis on uses of new technology. (p. 229)

Without specific planning and instruction, a school may exclude students with special learning needs, such as those with limited understanding of English, from fully participating in technology. Many schools' technology programs are geared toward students who learn faster and, thus, seldom encompass all students, no matter their ability level. Also, magnet schools, oftentimes not representative of all ethnic groups, must guard against omitting some types of students from information technology courses. Such omissions, even if accidental, raise the question of which groups get exclusive access to the most expensive and exciting new technology (Dowell and Raffel 1994).

New technologies should take into account the basic issues of diversity, including the need to learn a second language and how culture and race affect students in their day-to-day experiences. But teachers and administrators fail—through lack of expertise in computer technology—to draw up well-thought-out plans that make new programs accessible to all students. Course work that does not take into account such differences as students' lack of proficiency in English or their lack of access to computers outside school might only exacerbate old inequities in access (Dowell and Raffel 1994, 233). The learning community must ensure that its planning committee members have enough technological expertise to draw up a plan that balances access to technology with the school budget well enough to offer courses equitably, not to just a few students.

Further, Dowell and Raffel (1994) point out there can be significant differences in development of technological skills between students from families that own and regularly use computers and students from families that do not. Home access to electronic technology depends largely on whether a family can afford to pay for the hardware, software, and service fees. A learning community can reduce inequities springing from income by setting up programs to provide computer loans and computer training for parents who want or need such assistance. Helping parents and students develop skills and familiarity with computers and technology at home shows the learning community's support for continued education. The learning community should guarantee students access to technology no matter what the student's socioeconomic level.

BUDGETING, ACQUISITION, AND MAINTENANCE

Information technology is expensive to buy and maintain, thus it is important to develop a technology plan with a range of three to five years. Such a plan can remind the learning community to budget for new purchases and maintenance of existing equipment, both critical steps in developing and sustaining the use of technology. Tight budgets make it impossible for either districts or schools to buy all the state-of-the-art technology they could use. Districts and schools can stretch their money by tailoring purchases to their technology plans and the students' learning needs. Those that wish to make technological progress must make buying and maintaining equipment consistent and substantial line items in their budgets (Cushman 1994, 8).

Foundations and government agencies often make special grants available for schools to buy or lease computer-related equipment. But grants and regular budgets do not cover the enormous costs that schools must pay to buy and maintain up-to-date equipment. Too many schools buy advanced equipment without planning for its maintenance and other ongoing costs. It is not unusual to visit a school and find equipment collecting dust because the school or district failed to allocate money for maintenance or other types of support. Schools must guard against this trap by drawing up a clear maintenance plan, budgeting money to pay for it, and making maintenance part of the technology plan for the school and district (Barnett 1995).

Given these conditions, the principal has an important role in keeping the school focused on a well-developed technology plan that fits well with the district's plan. Clear budget allocation for purchases and maintenance of advanced equipment must be maintained at both the school and district levels, if technology is to improve students' achievement.

ADMINISTRATIVE USES OF TECHNOLOGY

Technological changes also offer the possibility of new approaches to administrative and managerial tasks. New technologies can provide more efficient and more effective ways to schedule classes; grade students; monitor student progress; keep records; communicate with teachers, parents, other community members, colleagues, and experts; develop information systems; network with other administrators; and handle other administrative tasks. Computers can quickly generate information to help guide a school's program planning and help the principal and other members of the learning community spot trends on a variety of topics. Electronic communications such as e-mail can help the school solve problems collaboratively, seek advice, and connect to other educational networks (Dowell and Raffel 1994, 231).

The principal must be aware of certain barriers to the use of technology and provide adequate support and resources to overcome these barriers. The principal should anticipate the need for more time for teachers to prepare new kinds of lessons; more time for teachers and students to experience meaningful work; additional people to train students and teachers in using new technology; financial support for professional development and for buying high-tech materials; and financial support to make on-site visits to learn more about exemplary programs. Even with the best of intentions, meaningful change will take at least five years, and a principal must be supportive during this lengthy process. A study by the Coalition of Essential Schools confirms that technological innovation and success depend on teachers having enough computers, support, and time, as well as a school structure and culture that encourage professional experimentation (Cushman 1994, 8).

To help implement new technology, the principal must be the school's leader in setting up partnerships with the business world that connect and enhance the work of technology in the learning community. Through connections with parents who may work in some technological industry, community business, or foundation, the principal and staff members can aid their school in its quest for continuing the development of technology. Here is where the learning community can expand its walls to the larger community and make the necessary connections for gaining knowledge and equipment, with the goal of educating students for the twenty-first century workforce.

Although the challenges of technology seem more daunting than dazzling to busy teachers and principals, the technological marketplace will become as commonplace and easy to use as the television and telephone. Cushman (1994) quotes Niguidula, who works on technological issues for the Coalition of Essential Schools, giving this perspective:

> Ten years from now, for instance, students or teachers researching something electronically will have no more trouble than they do using a library now. In the meantime, you can do a lot already if you're willing to invest a little time and effort. (p. 1)

For administrative personnel, technology can be divided into two areas, instructional and administrative, or managerial. Both aspects should focus on applications at the school level with district support. As the key person responsible for the administration of a technology plan, the principal should be knowledgeable of these aspects. The district, region, and state, as well as the private sector, should help support the development, implementation, and evaluation of individual schools' use of technology (CSDOE 1994). An example is California Assembly Bill 1470 setting up the Educational Technology Local Assistance Program to develop, implement, and evaluate uses of technology in professional development in schools. The bill calls for support from the district, region, state, and private sector (Dowell and Raffel 1994).

The instructional aspects of administering technology at the school level should focus on:

- Improving the quality and effectiveness of instruction and learning.
- Facilitating the integration of technology into the curriculum.
- Managing teaching resources more effectively through access to and use of technology.
- Evaluating the impact of technology on teaching and learning.

The administrative or management aspects of administering technology should concentrate on:

- Coordinating school-level planning for the use of technology.
- Ensuring that the school's use of technology meshes with district programs and planning.
- Using technology to manage the school more efficiently.
- Evaluating technology's impact on planning, use of resources, and management.

PROFESSIONAL DEVELOPMENT FOR TECHNOLOGY USE

Professional development is a crucial part of bringing a learning community's technology plan to fruition. Learning how to use technology effectively requires extensive professional development for most teachers, something that cannot be done in a single workshop. The school's infrastructure of support, learning, and sharing becomes vital as teachers, students, staff, and administrators together learn to use new technology. The use of technology becomes a learning process for the learning community and embodies the philosophy of a school learning together.

Outside training, support networks such as Apple's Christopher Columbus Consortium or Galaxy, university and business partnerships, site visitations, summer institutes, and other types of activities can provide professional development support. To infuse technology into all aspects of learning, teachers and principals need opportunities to spend time in an information-age environment and receive training on how to be effective facilitators of learning in a technology-rich setting (Dowell and Raffel 1994; Maurer and Davidson 1998). Teachers must have the opportunity to exchange experiences, solutions to problems, and innovative strategies with one another. They need to familiarize themselves with significant developments in learning and teaching through technology. For example, teachers are tapping electronic communications networks to trade assignments, coordinate student projects, plan and attend workshops, get information, collaborate with other professionals, apply for jobs, and ask advice (Cushman 1994). Many states offer statewide institutes in the form of teacher training academies, which focus on developing a corps of expert teachers to train other teachers on how to use and master technology. Those who receive the training can then pass these skills on to their students (Dowell and Raffel 1994).

Designing and implementing effective technology-based professional development should follow the concepts of professional development discussed in Chapter 8.

REFLECTIONS: AS A PRINCIPAL, YOU UNDERSTAND THE
RESEARCH AND BEST PRACTICES IN PROFESSIONAL DEVELOP-
MENT; HOW WOULD YOU HELP FACILITATE AND DESIGN A TECH-
NOLOGY PROFESSIONAL DEVELOPMENT PLAN FOR YOUR
SCHOOL? WRITE DOWN YOUR THOUGHTS.

CONFIGURATIONS

The configurations of technology, within a learning community and district, need to be addressed in the school and district technology plans. As the problem scenario at the beginning of this chapter asked: Has the school's technology planning been helter-skelter, with no rhyme or reason as to the selection and placement of equipment? What are the standards for placing technology equipment—TVs, VCRs, cable hookups, telephones, computers—in each classroom? Are there computer labs, policies for lending technology equipment to classrooms, specialized technology classrooms, schoolwide networking, access to satellite dishes, faxes, and so on? These are important questions in the discussion of configuring technology within a learning community. Further, how does all this relate to the district's technology plan?

Setting up networks throughout the school and district is important and enables students and staff to have access to their work from anywhere in the school or district. Everyone in the learning community should be able to connect to the library and other information resources, and teachers should be able to access student records through a central data system. Linking classrooms to other schools, the district, businesses, and information centers, such as university libraries or electronic bulletin boards, enables the learning community to draw on the most up-to-date learning resources.

What technology does the school library have? Is there a library media teacher to help students and teachers use and manage information resources and technology? Can teleconferencing be used for learning in the school? As technological devices become less expensive and easier to use, their implementation will be less obtrusive as they are introduced to the school. District and school technology planning with various configurations based on sound research and effective practice can make a difference for student achievement and teacher practices. A learning community working with the district on configurations of technology can develop the optimum technology usage for the school.

IMPLEMENTATION

The implementation of technology within a learning community is crucial. It is the implementation of the technology plan that sees the enactment of all the planning. Implementation is an ongoing process as new technologies and phases of the technology plan are developed. Individuals must be apprised of the technology implementation process so that they clearly understand and use the technology that is being placed in the school.

EVALUATION AND REVISION

The final piece of technology planning is to evaluate the implementation of the school's technology plan and make revisions as needed. The school technology committee should create a clear evaluation process for ongoing review by the committee and the rest of the learning community. Setting up evaluation in advance permits data to be captured as needed. Each evaluation should lead to a revision of the technology plan. Too often, schools develop technology plans but fail to implement them properly or set up an evaluation process that can help the school adequately judge the plan's success. Evaluation and revision of the technology plan will help keep the plan up-to-date and meaningful for the learning community.

SUMMARY

The role of technology in today's learning community is that of a vital instructional and administrative tool. All members of the learning community must have the opportunity to acquire the knowledge and skills, from basic to highly technical, they need to adapt to emerging new technologies. Through thoughtful planning, the learning community can provide for access and equity to a variety of technologies for students, teachers, staff, parents, and the rest of the community. The learning community, led by the principal, can use technology to reach the school's vision: improving student achievement and services.

REFLECTIVE ACTIVITIES

1. Applying Technology Planning in a Learning Community

Apply the technology planning areas from this chapter (listed in Figure 10.1) to your school setting. What insights have you gained after reviewing each area? What would you change or expand in each area for your school?

2. Instructional and Administrative Technology Use in Your School

Analyze the use of technology within your school, in both the instructional and administrative aspects. What are your conclusions?

SUGGESTED READINGS

Cushman, Kathleen, ed. 1994. Technology in the Essential School: Making Change in the Information Age. *Horace* 10(3), 1–8. Providence, RI: Coalition of Essential Schools.

Fisher, Charles, David C. Dwyer, and Keith Yocam, eds. 1996. *Education and Technology: Reflections on Computing in Classrooms.* San Francisco: Jossey-Bass.

Knapp, Linda Roehrig, and Allen D. Glenn. 1996. *Restructuring School with Technology.* Boston: Allyn and Bacon.

Maurer, Matthew M., and George S. Davidson. 1998. *Leadership in Instructional Technology.* Upper Saddle River, NJ: Merrill/Prentice Hall.

O'Neil, John. 1995. Technology Schools: A Conversation with Chris Dede. *Educational Leadership* 53(2), 6–12.

REFERENCES

Apple Classrooms of Tomorrow (ACOT). 1993. *Apple Classrooms of Tomorrow, Stevens Creek Elementary School.* Cupertino, CA: Apple Computer.

Barnett, Harvey. 1995. *Presentation Planning Technology—Successful Strategies.* March 1995. Cupertino, CA: Cupertino Union School District. Unpublished paper.

Bradsher, Monica, and Lucy Hagen. 1995. The Kids Network: Student-Scientists Pool Resources. *Educational Leadership* 53(2): 38–43.

California State Department of Education (CSDOE). 1994. *Building the Future: K–12 Network Technology Planning Guide.* Sacramento: CSDOE.

Collins, Allen. 1991. The Role of Computer Technology in Restructuring Schools. *Phi Delta Kappan* 73(1): 28–36.

Committee on Instructional Technology. 1970. *To Improving Learning: A Report to the President and Congress of the United States*, 5. Washington, DC: U.S. Government Printing Office 40–7105.

Cushman, Kathleen, ed. 1994. Technology in the Essential School: Making Change in the Information Age. *Horace* 10(3): 1–8. Providence, RI: Coalition of Essential Schools.

Data for the National Education Goals Report. 1995. Vol. 1. *National Data 1994.* Washington, DC: U.S. Government Printing Office.

Dowell, Carol, and Lisa Raffel, eds. 1994. *The Unfinished Journey: Restructuring Schools in a Diverse Society.* San Francisco: California Tomorrow.

Dwyer, David, Cathy Ringstaff, and Judy Sandholtz. 1991. Changes in Teachers' Beliefs and Practices in Technology-Rich Classrooms. *Educational Leadership* 48(8): 45–52.

Heinich, Robert, Michael Molenda, James D. Russell, and Sharon E. Smaldino. 1996. *Instructional Media and Technologies for Learning.* 5th ed. Upper Saddle River, NJ: Merrill/Prentice Hall.

Knapp, Linda Roehrig, and Allen D. Glenn. 1996. *Restructuring School with Technology.* Boston: Allyn and Bacon.

Maurer, Matthew M., and George S. Davidson. 1998. *Leadership in Instructional Technology.* Upper Saddle River, NJ: Merrill/Prentice Hall.

Murray, David R., and Meg Murray. 1994. Harnessing Technology: Teaching and Learning in the Future Tense. Chap. 12 in *Field Guide to Educational Renewal: Vermont Restructuring Collaborative,* edited by William Mathis. Brandon, VT: Holistic Education Press.

O'Neil, John. 1995. Technology Schools: A Conversation with Chris Dede. *Educational Leadership* 53(2): 6–12.

Weiler, Berman. 1988. *Restructuring California Education: A Design for Public Education in the 21st Century.* Berkeley: Berman Weiler Associates.

Willis, Bernice H., Sheila N. Thomas, and Michael H. Hoppe. 1985. *Teaching and Learning: Changing Minds in a Changing World.* Research Triangle Park, NC: Southeastern Regional Council for Educational Improvement.

Zimmerman, Joy. 1992. Moving Technology into Education: Is It a Fit? *Far West Focus On Changing School Practice* (October): 1–8. San Francisco: Far West Laboratory for Educational Research and Development.

CHAPTER 11

CHANGE

PROBLEM SCENARIO

Αs the principal, you must deal with constant change and continuous efforts to improve the school. You are responsible for orchestrating the school improvements designed to ensure increasing success for all students. Everyone—teachers, staff, parents, and the rest of the community—expects the best education for students. How does a learning community continue to change and improve for all students? As the principal, what do you need to know about the change process to bring about systemic and sustained change in your school? What plans would you make to facilitate the change process in your learning community?

THE PROBLEMS OF CHANGE EFFORTS IN SCHOOLS

The school is not now a learning organization. Irregular waves of change, episodic projects, fragmentation of effort, and grinding overload [are] the lot of most schools. The vast majority of change efforts are misconceived because they fail to understand and harness the combined forces of moral purpose and skilled change agentry.[1]

Initiating, carrying out, and institutionalizing changes in a learning community do not simply happen without effort. Each school and district must continually work to meet the challenge of making improvements to achieve success for all students. Improving a school and developing a learning community require change. The change process demands that individuals, the school organization, and the local school community accept change, adapt to it, and cooperate in institutionalizing it.

School change is not an easy task; it takes time, planning, and ongoing support to institutionalize change (Fullan 1991). It is far easier to maintain and follow traditional practices and familiar routines of schooling. The challenge for every principal is to bring about change that will last and make a real difference in the quality of learning and life for students, teachers, and the rest of the learning community. Too often a principal comes to a new school full of ideas for changes, which may parallel the agendas of the superintendent and board of education. After several years of hard work, however, the principal finds that none of these ideas has become institutionalized in the school. Why haven't the changes that the principal perceives are needed been realized?

In fact, schools have not really changed much over the past century. Each attempt at educational innovation generally slips back into a traditional mode of educational operation that is safe and familiar. Why is it so difficult for schools to change? Visit any school and talk with any teachers, and you will likely hear them retrace a long history of attempts at innovation, with a long list of educational programs that school personnel enthusiastically supported in hopes of improving education for their students. But you may not hear much about changes that worked and made a difference. Real change in schools remains elusive.

This chapter addresses the change process and the principal's role in continuous school improvement. It will explore the issues of sustainable, systemic change that can survive the departure of the initiating principal and become part of the learning community's culture.

LEARNING FROM PAST LESSONS ABOUT EDUCATIONAL CHANGE

Sarason (1990) in *The Predictable Failure of School Reform* contends that the chronic failure of school reform is not in the ideas themselves,

[1] Reprinted with permission of Falmer Press from *Change Forces: Probing the Depths of Educational Reform*, 42, by Michael Fullan. © 1993 by Falmer Press.

but in the implementation of those ideas. Sarason says there is a true misunderstanding of how individuals and schools change. Educators, especially principals who have the responsibility for orchestrating change within their schools, must study the change process. Sarason (1990) makes the following three important points regarding change.

1. OUTSIDERS AND INSIDERS MUST BE INVOLVED IN THE CHANGE EFFORTS

Significant change requires the involvement of insiders—teachers, staff, administrators within the school or district—as well as outsiders—parents, business, and community. Change cannot happen unless all stakeholders are involved. Most change efforts start and stop within the school, involving only teachers and staff, without anyone ever seeking input from other important members of the learning community. Educators often ask for token input from the outsiders, but then go ahead with what they, the insiders, want. Thus, change fails because outsiders cannot understand the innovation, see its educational value, or provide assistance with implementing it.

2. POWER RELATIONSHIPS MUST SHIFT

There must be a shift in power relationships if schools are to change for the better. There must be a balance of power inside and outside the school for educational innovations to be effective and lasting. The principal, teachers, district administrators, and board members cannot be the only arbiters of what is best for students' education. Many individuals and organizations outside the school must share power and input into important educational decisions for change. Until these power shifts take place, the insiders—principals and teachers—will only be spinning their wheels in hopes of institutionalizing changes within the learning community. The outsiders—parents and community members—can block or influence educational change, especially if they have had no involvement in the change process.

3. WORKING AND LEARNING CONDITIONS MUST CHANGE

Teachers, students, and staff members must have better working and learning conditions for change. They must have time for thoughtful discussion and learning about the best practices for education. An in-service training workshop may introduce a new concept, such as cooperative education or early literacy strategies, but teachers must have the opportunity to discuss, practice, and support one another when they carry such concepts back to the classroom. Conditions within the school and classroom must support ongoing learning for teachers and the principal with time, structure, recognition, and resources.

Thus, a central task for the principal is creating and fostering a culture within the school that develops collaborative working relationships for change between teachers, teachers and principal, teachers and parents, and teachers and community (Hargreaves 1997). Principals must study the points made by Sarason (1990), as discussed in the preceding paragraphs, to facilitate the change process for schools.

REFLECTIONS: AS A NEW PRINCIPAL, HOW WOULD YOU REACT TO

SARASON'S IDEAS ON THE FAILURE OF SCHOOL REFORMS IN TRY-

ING TO BRING CHANGE TO IMPROVE STUDENT SUCCESS IN YOUR

SCHOOL? THINK ABOUT THEM AND WRITE DOWN YOUR IDEAS.

THE CHANGE PROCESS

Change is an ongoing process, not an event. Change does not just happen one day. Trying to get people to change the way they do things requires an understanding of the challenges and difficulties one can expect to face. The blank stares, foot-dragging, and other subtle forms of resistance can be seen in any school, district, or organization going through change. John Kenneth Galbraith (1972) describes a typical reaction to change:

> Faced with the choice between changing one's mind and proving that there is no need to do so, almost everybody gets busy on the proof. (p. 10)

Galbraith's comment applies directly to any principal dealing with the change process within the school. The principal must understand the change process, if improvements are to be made and institutionalized.

Principals and district administrators often fail to study the process of change and plan for all aspects of change. Today, change is the name of the game in schools attempting to meet the learning needs of their diverse student population. Schools that cannot deal effectively with change will fail to meet the needs of students or the community as a whole. One need only look at the increasing dropout rate or the illiteracy rate of our society to see that education has not met the needs of all students. Schools must be continuously engaged in the process of change or they will not be successful with their students and the ever-changing needs of society.

New perspectives on the difficulties of implementing the change process are both useful and important to understand. As Fullan (1993) puts it:

> It is only by raising our consciousness and insights about the totality of educational change that we can do something about it. (p. 16)

Without discussion of the change process, the people involved will not understand the power or the problems that change can create. Understanding the dynamics and implications of change becomes a powerful means for the successful implementation of an educational innovation by a principal and the learning community. Most schools study the issues surrounding the educational innovation—for example, introducing the whole-language approach or hands-on math or science—without studying the change process itself. Schools tend to spend little time understanding what happens to individuals and the learning community when change takes place (Fullan 1991). The following key questions can serve as a guide in studying and preparing for the change process to make it smoother and more successful:

Key Questions for the Change Process

- What is the school vision—the collective vision of the school learning community?
- Who are the stakeholders?
- What are the skills or capacities needed to make the change?
- What are the incentives or motivations to change?
- What resources are available to make the change?
- What are the politics of change? How might the change involve board members, teachers' and classified unions, or other community members?
- What is the action plan for change?
- How are transitions managed for individuals and organizations during the change process?
- What modifications should be made during the change process or implementation of the action plan?
- How will the action plan for change be reviewed, evaluated, and revised?

These key questions are presented graphically in the Change Process Model (see Figure 11.1). This model can help a principal visualize what must happen for change to take place in a successful way. Each question must be addressed by the individuals with the responsibility of managing the change, typically, the principal, leadership team, and teachers.

As Goodlad (1990) describes it:

> If schools are to become the responsive, renewing institutions that they must, teachers in them must be purposefully engaged in the renewal process. (p. 10)

The principal must ensure the involvement of teachers and others in the change process. The principal must enlarge the circle of peo-

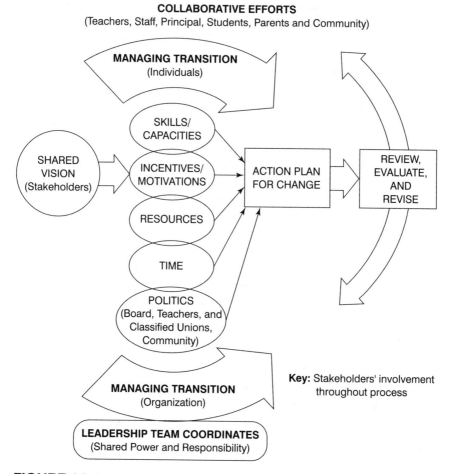

FIGURE 11.1
Change Process Model

ple responsible for implementing change. The circle must certainly include teachers, but also people outside the school, especially parents, members of the business community, and the community at large.

The Change Process Model (Figure 11.1) starts with a thorough discussion of the school vision. Vision in a learning community is not the principal's personal goals but the collective vision of the community that develops over time and becomes the heart and passion of what the school is about. This vision, with its underlying principles, values, and beliefs about students, should drive the need for the skills, capacity, incentives, motivations, and resources to bring about a lasting change.

As an example of applying the Change Process Model, assume that a learning community decides to improve reading instruction in the school. The principal and the rest of the learning community should address the following key questions when preparing to implement this change, based on the Change Process Model in Figure 11.1:

- What is the school's vision for improving reading instruction?
- How are the stakeholders involved in the creation of the vision and the change process?
- What reading skills, techniques, or what capacities, such as professional development, are needed to teach reading to today's students, given the most recent research on effective teaching of reading?
- What motivation or other incentive will help teachers want to change their current practices of teaching reading?
- What resources and time are available for teachers who wish to change their techniques of teaching reading?
- What politics are involved in changing reading instruction? In what ways should we involve board members, teachers' and classified unions, parents, and others in the community?
- How are each of the teachers, principal, parents, and other individuals managing the transition to the vision for reading instruction within the school?
- How is the learning community—the organization—managing the transition from old ways of teaching reading to the new ways?
- What is the action plan for change for the reading program at the school?
- How will this action plan be reviewed, evaluated, and revised on a regular basis to include adjustments to ensure the lasting success of the new program within the learning community? How will we know when the new reading program is successful? What adaptations do we

need to make, given the ongoing analysis of our progress with the new reading program?

REFLECTIONS: AFTER REVIEWING THESE QUESTIONS REGARDING

THE CHANGE PROCESS, WHAT INSIGHTS HAVE YOU GAINED IN

IMPLEMENTING CHANGES? HOW OFTEN DO PRINCIPALS AND

SCHOOLS LOOK AT EACH ASPECT OF THE CHANGE PROCESS AND

PLAN FOR EACH? IF YOU WERE TO REVIEW EACH QUESTION RAISED

BY THE CHANGE PROCESS MODEL BASED ON A RECENT CHANGE

IN YOUR SCHOOL, WHICH ISSUES WERE ADDRESSED AND WHICH

WERE NOT? HOW DOES THE CHANGE PROCESS MODEL HELP YOU

PLAN FOR CHANGE? WRITE DOWN YOUR THOUGHTS.

The Change Process Model emphasizes the importance of dealing with helping individuals—teachers, staff members, students, parents, and community members—as well as the entire school organization cope with change. The next two sections will address transition for the individual and the organization.

MANAGING THE TRANSITION FOR INDIVIDUALS

Failure to personalize the change process by managing the transition for each individual can lead to disaster for individuals and the school and will result in little institutionalized change. Educators must address personal issues and concerns during the change process, giving each individual time to develop a clear understanding of the effects of change on each player in the process.

Bridges (1991) states:

> You will be unable to get the results you need without getting into "that personal stuff." (p. 5)

Fullan (1993) reinforces the importance of the individual educator as the critical starting point. The efforts of individual educators can increase the leverage for change, giving those educators control over what they do. In a learning community, the principal and each and every teacher has a responsibility to help create a school capable of continuous inquiry and self-renewal. Each and every educator must strive to be an effective agent of change (Fullan 1993). It is only from individuals taking action to alter their current situation that the school will undergo sustained change. A principal must help recognize and facilitate the change process for each member of the learning community.

If change is to take place, individuals must stop doing things the old way and start doing things a new way. There is no way to do that impersonally—only individual by individual accepting the change. According to Bridges (1991), the key is dealing with the transition, or the internal psychological reorientation, of an individual coming to terms with change (see Figure 11.2). Transition management is a way of understanding the internal turmoil every person experiences with a change and of helping each person feel more comfortable with the process of change. Managing individual transition means helping each person in the school develop a reorientation. Individuals need to develop new mindsets, new outlooks, and new identities when dealing with change. Old ways of doing things must end and the new must take hold, if the change is to become permanent. The only way to sustain change is through managing the transition of each individual from the old to the new. The principal must continually be thinking of ways to help individuals with the transition as a part of the overall change efforts.

As Figure 11.2 illustrates, the term **transition** refers to the personal, internal, psychological reorientation that an individual goes through in coping with change, whereas **change** refers to the external event—a new principal or superintendent, a new reading technique or new policy, new team roles, or a new school site. Unless transition takes place at the individual level, change will not work.

FIGURE 11.2
Change and Transition

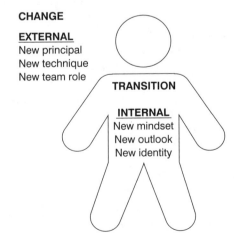

CHANGE

EXTERNAL
New principal
New technique
New team role

TRANSITION

INTERNAL
New mindset
New outlook
New identity

REFLECTIONS: CAN YOU THINK OF EXAMPLES OF AN ATTEMPTED

CHANGE THAT DID NOT TAKE HOLD BECAUSE THE INDIVIDUALS

INVOLVED DID NOT REALLY WANT IT, UNDERSTAND IT, OR ACCEPT

IT? YOUR OWN EXPERIENCES IN A CHANGE PROCESS ARE IMPOR-

TANT LESSONS TO REFLECT ON AS YOU STUDY THE CHANGE

PROCESS. TAKE TIME TO THINK ABOUT YOUR EXPERIENCES WITH

CHANGE IN YOUR SCHOOL. WRITE DOWN YOUR THOUGHTS.

The principal and the rest of the learning community cannot deal with change without seriously studying and implementing a change process model. Members of a learning community know the road to change is difficult but not impossible, especially if each individual develops a clear understanding of change and accepts the transition to the new. Change should never be attempted merely for the sake of change. The change process must entail serious and well-thought-out plans that include a successful transition for each individual. People often learn about a change from an announcement, unaccompanied by plans to help them make the transition and come to terms with the change.

As Bridges (1991) puts it:

> It isn't the changes that do you in, it's the transitions. (p. 3)

Transition management is one of the most important techniques a principal should acquire for implementing any change within a learning community. As mentioned, Bridges (1991) describes transition as the internal psychological process people go through to come to terms with a new situation—for example, whole-language instruction, multigraded classes, or thematic integrated instruction. Unless transition occurs, the change will not work. As the saying goes: "The more things change, the more they stay the same." A school can make any number of changes, but without the successful transitions of the individuals involved, nothing will be different after the dust settles. People need to go through the transition, within the change process, and come to terms with new ideas that bring about the change. As an example, a reading teacher must go through a personal transition from using certain reading instruction techniques to learning and adopting new and more effective reading practices.

Hord (1987) employed the Concern-Based Adoption Model to describe the changing feelings of individuals as they learn about a proposed change, prepare to use it, and modify it as a result. These individual transition levels represent the general kind of development that takes place as an individual adopts changes. The seven stages of the model, along with typical concerns at each stage, are:

1. Awareness—I am not concerned about it.
2. Informational—I would like to know more about it.
3. Personal—How will using it affect me?
4. Management—I seem to be spending all my time getting material ready.
5. Consequence—How is my use affecting kids?
6. Collaboration—I am concerned about relating what I am doing with what other teachers are doing.
7. Refocusing—I have some ideas about something that would work even better. (p. 101)

The principal can use this model as a framework to identify the concerns of individuals at various stages and match transition strategies with these levels of concern. Recognizing the progress of individuals as they make the transition to accepting and adopting a change is important for the principal and the rest of the learning community as they strive for continuous school improvement.

Transition management is the starting point not the outcome of change. The first step in transition is actually an ending, leaving behind old ways of doing things. Psychological transition depends on individuals letting go of the reality and identity they have before the change takes place. In a school undergoing change, each teacher must let go of old realities and identities to accept the new way of doing things. Nothing undermines a school change as much as the failure to think through who will have to let go of what when change occurs. Change does not just happen. School change must be facilitated by the principal working in a collaborative effort with teachers, individually and in teams.

Sizer (1991) describes typical reactions to change in education and the need for a clear transition plan to bring about the educational change:

> [The public's and parents'] criticism, even when offered lovingly, is often greeted paradoxically: responsible people agree with [the criticism], but also agree to do little to address the failings. Reform is for someone else's school. We're happy with the one we have, and we are skeptical of any effort to alter it. It is no wonder that there has been so little change. (pp. 10–11)

Since transition begins with ending old ways, the principal must plan to deal with those endings. It is important to remember that individuals do not like endings. The principal and other teachers, staff members, parents, and community members responsible for the educational change must plan the transition so the changes do not become unmanageable. As a leader of the school, the principal, with the help of the leadership team, must plan how to end what used to be, for example, in making a change from basal readers to a whole-language approach. In facing the ending of old ways, teachers may fear losing their familiar turf within the classroom and school, their routines and techniques, and even their sense of self. Most individuals will resist not the change itself—a new curriculum, instructional strategy, or procedure—but these personal losses and endings. It does no good at this stage to talk about the wonderful outcomes of an educational change. This is the time to deal directly with the inevitable sense of loss that individuals will feel during the transition to the new educational idea or technique. What steps will help individuals overcome their sense of loss so they can make the transition to new educational ideas? Following are key questions to help the principal and the rest of the learning community generate a plan to help individuals make a smooth transition.

Key Questions to Help Individuals Overcome a Sense of Loss in Transition

1. What will end because of the change?
2. Who will lose what with the change?
3. How do individuals accept the reality and importance of their losses due to the change?
4. How does a leadership team recognize individual and group losses to help the transition?
5. How can you help individuals not overreact to change?
6. Do individuals understand the proposed change?
7. How will information be communicated during the transition?
8. What plan is there to celebrate progress in the transition?

Answering these key questions will help the principal, leadership team, and the entire community better understand the change itself and how the transition process will work. This process will enable individuals within the learning community to understand the change and develop common values, goals, and plans. The change plan itself should evolve and allow for the use of many individual talents. Change plans cannot be fixed, but must be fluid to allow for adaptations as the learning community sees the need arise. Those responsible must make modifications to meet individuals' need during the transition so that the change becomes permanent.

As Sergiovanni (1996) describes it:

Change will become more of a way of life for teachers and less a planned occasion. (p. 167)

Change must take place to keep the school vital and responsive to its constituents' needs. Planning and carrying out the change must be done as a whole as well as individually. The need for planned and monitored change that deals with individuals within the school is a critical element in the change process that a principal must understand and deal with daily as a school makes the transition.

As Bridges (1991) puts it:

The single biggest reason organizational changes fail is that no one thought about endings or planned to manage their impact on people. (p. 32)

Through a learning community's focus on transition planning, continuous change can occur and become institutionalized within the school. A learning community provides opportunities for inquiry and reflection about practices on a continual basis, thus providing opportunities to make and process the changes. Principals should heed the warning of McLaughlin and Talbert (1993) and reflect on their transition planning for change:

Effecting and enabling the teacher learning required by systemic reform cannot be accomplished through traditional staff development models-episodic, decontextualized injections of "knowledge" and technique. The path to change in the classroom core lies within and through teachers' professional communities: learning communities which generate knowledge, craft new norms of practice, and sustain participants in their efforts to reflect, examine, experiment, and change. (p. 18)

When a learning community develops a transition process for teachers, staff, students, parents, and the rest of the community, the process holds promise for real reform in schools. The following list summarizes important facts for the principal to remember about change in the learning community (Fullan 1993):

- Change is a process, not an event.
- Change takes time (four to seven years for sustained institutionalized change).
- Change is accomplished by individuals.

- Change is a highly personal experience for each individual.
- Change involves developmental growth for each individual allowing an internal transition.
- Change facilitation should focus on individuals, innovations, and context as well as the whole organization.

MANAGING THE TRANSITION FOR THE ORGANIZATION

The Change Process Model (Figure 11.1) emphasizes not only the importance of the individual in transition, but also the role of the school organization. Plans for change must consider the school organization as a whole. This is the larger, system view that must be considered. It is the system that creates the dynamic interactions—the skills/capacities, incentives/motivations, resources, time, politics, leadership team, stakeholders. These parts are interactive components within a change process for a school organization. Managing the transition of the school as a whole takes planning. Using the key questions from the previous section to answer issues that face the entire school organization will help the change process. This system of interaction among various people in the organization and the change process is critical if change is to be adopted, implemented, and institutionalized within a school. Thus, the principal must plan for organizational as well as individual transitions.

A collaborative leadership team working with the principal and faculty can help with the change efforts. As facilitators of change in the transition process, leadership team members can embody new practices, disseminate information, cheer the efforts of others, and provide support (Hord et al. 1987). The principal must help the organization's change efforts by enlisting the support and help of a variety of individuals. Principals must remember that change will not happen simply because they want it to.

Evans' (1996) model for Paradigms of Change illustrates the difference between a systemic approach to change and a rational-structural approach (see Figure 11.3). Principals should view their school with a systemic perspective as they plan the organizational transition. The systemic model recognizes the fluid, psychological aspects of the organization, a pragmatic approach to planning, a view of innovation as a process, a focus on meaning, and implementation designed to build commitment and purpose.

Principals need to comprehend the differences in these two views of change—**rational-structural** and **systemic**—if they are to under-

	Rational-Structural	**Systemic**
Environment	stable predictable	turbulent unpredictable
Organization	stable logical	fluid psychological
Planning	objective, linear long-range	pragmatic, adaptable medium-range
Innovation	product fixed outcome	process emerging outcome
Focus	structure, function task, roles, rules	people, culture meaning, motivation
Implementation	almost purely top-down disseminating, pressuring	top-down and bottom-up commitment-building, purposing

FIGURE 11.3
Paradigms of Change

Reprinted with permission of Jossey-Bass Inc. from *The Human Side of School Change: Reform, Resistance, and the Real Life Problems of Innovation*, p. 7, by Robert Evans. © 1996 by Jossey-Bass Inc., Publishers.

stand the change process. The traditional rational-structural perspective explains how organizations ought to work, but fails to account for why they often don't, and why the same kinds of problems arise over and over (Bolman and Deal 1991, 36). A systemic view allows a school organization to understand change as it occurs. A systemic perspective allows a principal to see change as a process with emerging outcomes that focuses on people, meaning, and commitment to improve the learning community.

BASIC LESSONS ON THE COMPLEXITY OF CHANGE

Fullan (1993) reminds us of the complexity of the change process by providing eight basic lessons of the new paradigm of change (Figure 11.4). The principal and teachers initiating change within a school should study these lessons to inform their planning and actions during the change process. These lessons about change help individuals understand what change entails and why it is not easy. Hopefully, these lessons can serve as a reminder during the change process for the learning community.

---

1. **You Can't Mandate What Matters**

   (The more complex the change, the less you can force it.)

2. **Change Is a Journey, Not a Blueprint**

   (Change is nonlinear, loaded with uncertainty and excitement and sometimes perverse.)

3. **Problems Are Our Friends**

   (Problems are inevitable, and you can't learn without them.)

4. **Vision and Strategic Planning Come Later**

   (Premature visions and planning blind.)

5. **Individualism and Collectivism Must Have Equal Power**

   (There are no one-sided solutions to isolation and group-think.)

6. **Neither Centralization Nor Decentralization Works**

   (Both top-down and bottom-up strategies are necessary.)

7. **Connection with the Wider Environment Is Critical for Success**

   (The best organizations learn externally as well as internally.)

8. **Every Person Is a Change Agent**

   (Change is too important to leave to the experts—personal mindset and mastery are the ultimate protection.)

FIGURE 11.4
Fullan's Basic Lessons of the New Paradigm of Change

Reprinted with permission of Falmer Press from *Change Forces: Probing the Depths of Educational Reform,* pp. 21–22, by Michael Fullan. © 1993 by Falmer Press.

SUMMARY

Change may be the destination a new educational idea, but helping individuals understand the need for a change makes it possible. Deliberate planning with individuals as well as the organization will make a major difference in how the change is implemented and how long it will persist. The Change Process Model can be a guide for change within a learning community. The principal and the rest of the learning community can use the model to their benefit as they develop and implement ideas for school improvement. The change process affords the entire learning community an opportunity to inquire and reflect, make the transition, implement the change, and reflect and revise their change plans for school improvement on a continual basis.

REFLECTIVE ACTIVITIES

1. Analyzing a Change Process

Define and analyze a recent change that took place at your school. Using the Change Process Model (Figure 11.1), how would you analyze each aspect? What insights have you gained about the change process?

2. Applying the Change Process Model

Take a current educational idea that you wish to implement within your school and apply the Change Process Model (Figure 11.1). How would you plan for the individual and organization transition using each of the model's parts? Prepare a change plan to share with others in class.

SUGGESTED READINGS

Bridges, William. 1991. *Managing Transitions: Making the Most of Change*. Reading, MA: Addison-Wesley.

Evans, Robert. 1996. *The Human Side of School Change: Reform, Resistance, and the Real-Life Problems of Innovation*. San Francisco: Jossey-Bass.

Fullan, Michael. 1991. *The New Meaning of Educational Change*. 2d ed. New York: Teachers College Press.

Fullan, Michael. 1993. *Change Forces: Probing the Depths of Educational Reform*. New York: Falmer Press.

Hargreaves, Andrew, ed. 1997. *Rethinking Educational Change with Heart and Mind*. Alexandria, VA: Association for Supervision and Curriculum Development.

REFERENCES

Bolman, Lee G., and Terrence E. Deal. 1991. *Reframing Organizations*. San Francisco: Jossey-Bass.

Bridges, William. 1991. *Managing Transitions: Making the Most of Change*. Reading, MA: Addison-Wesley.

Evans, Robert. 1996. *The Human Side of School Change: Reform, Resistance, and the Real-Life Problems of Innovation*. San Francisco: Jossey-Bass.

Fullan, Michael. 1991. *The New Meaning of Educational Change*. 2d ed. New York: Teachers College Press.

Fullan, Michael. 1993. *Change Forces: Probing the Depths of Educational Reform*. New York: Falmer Press.

Goodlad, John. 1990. *Teachers for Our Nation's Schools*. San Francisco: Jossey-Bass.

Hargreaves, Andrew, ed. 1997. *Rethinking Educational Change with Heart and Mind*. Alexandria, VA: Association for Supervision and Curriculum Development.

Hord, Shirley M. 1987. *Evaluating Educational Innovation*. London: Croom Helm Ltd.

Hord, Shirley M., William L. Rutherford, Leslie Huling-Austin, and Gene E. Hall. 1987. *Taking Charge of Change*. Alexandria, VA: Association for Supervision and Curriculum Development.

McLaughlin, Milbrey, and Joan E. Talbert. 1993. *Contexts That Matter for Teaching and Learning*. Palo Alto, CA: Stanford University, Center for Research on the Context of Secondary Teaching.

Sarason, Seymour B. 1990. *The Predictable Failure of School Reform*. San Francisco: Jossey-Bass.

Sergiovanni, Thomas J. 1996. *Leadership for the Schoolhouse*. San Francisco: Jossey-Bass.

Sizer, Theodore R. 1991. *Horace's School*. Boston: Houghton Mifflin.

INDEX